LIVING

with a

MAN

in

TWO
WORLDS

PAM STONE

LIVING

with a

MAN

in

TWO
WORLDS

LIVING WITH A MAN IN TWO WORLDS
Published by Voice of Evangelism Outreach Ministries
P. O. Box 3595
Cleveland, TN 37320
423.478.3456
www.perrystone.org

Scripture quotations marked NKJV are from the New King James Version of the Bible. Copyright © 1979, 1980, 1982 by Thomas Nelson, Inc., publishers. Used by permission.

Scripture quotations marked KJV are from the King James Version of the Bible.

Cover design and layout by Michael Dutton

First edition printed 2013
Printed in the United States of America
ISBN 978-0-9785920-1-1

CONTENTS

Foreword   7

Introduction   9

Part One: In the Beginning

Chapter 1: I Almost Didn't Make It   15

Chapter 2: The Early Years   23

Chapter 3: Wanted: A Preacher   33

Part Two: Life After Marriage

Chapter 4: Life in Cleveland, Tennessee   41

Chapter 5: Our Children   47

Chapter 6: A Man Who Lives in Two Worlds   57

Chapter 7: Sweating Peanuts in a Controversy   65

Chapter 8: Hearing the Voice of the Lord   83

Part Three: Manna-Fest and Beyond

Chapter 9: The Inside Story of Manna-fest   97

Chapter 10: Mama P and Papa P   117

Chapter 11: I'm Not Going to be a Farmer's Wife   125

Chapter 12: The Perry You Might not Know   141

Chapter 13: Questions You Have Asked   151

Conclusion   175

FOREWORD

Being the minister in the family, I am the one who normally shares personal stories to encourage congregations and build their faith. I am thrilled that Pam has finally put in writing many personal narratives of her life, as well as her perspective of the ministry.

Since April of 1982, when we were united in marriage, each issue of the Voice of Evangelism magazine has featured an article called *Pam's Corner*. According to many of our ministry partners, this is the first article they read when the magazine arrives. Over the past several years, the ministry has received e-mails, primarily from women, who ask Pam various personal questions such as: What are the benefits of home schooling? How are ministry finances spent? What is it like being married to a minister? How are we supposed to raise our children in a secular America that is increasingly hostile to Christianity?

Most people who have followed our ministry for many years have heard my stories—or at least my version of events—as they relate to meeting and marrying Pam. However, she has viewed this journey through her own eyes. I have a policy to never counsel people, as I believe a minister should have specific academic credentials for this process. Pam, on the other hand, has spent hours with close friends in their times of grief, sorrow, disappointment and spiritual struggle, and has given them wisdom to resolve matters. At times I would be sitting at home and hear her on the phone, quoting entire sections of a message I had preached. She stored the message in her memory and had the confidence to share God's truth with the hurting.

One of Pam's favorite statements is, "Let's make memories." Pam loves pictures and we have cabinets filled with albums to prove it. At times I pull out an album that dates back to the time we were married, and I begin to reminisce of those wonderful, early days of ministry, when life was simple and we traveled from state to state, spending weeks in a pastor's home or, as we did on one occasion, seventy-seven days in the same small hotel room. Many times I have opened a large photo album and turned the pages to a snapshot of her with her long hair and that smooth, baby-like complexion (which she still has) and said to myself, "No wonder you married Pam. She's a knockout!"

I have been a most fortunate and blessed man to have met her in 1980, walked her down the aisle as Pam Taylor, and left the altar with her as Pam Stone. I know that she was hand-picked by God from the foundation of the earth, to enter this world and become the rose of my life. It would take a special woman to do all that she has done and continues to do in faithful service to the Lord. In all of our marriage, I have never heard her complain about the ministry or about the long hours required to complete the many tasks.

I am so happy, as her charming, tall, handsome, intelligent husband (I *had* to say that) to endorse the first—and perhaps the only book—she will ever write. Get your coffee or tea, sit back and relax, and join her in her journal of a journey—the ministry from her perspective.

Love you always Pam,
Perry

INTRODUCTION

In this journey of life, each one of us makes memories that will become stories that are passed down from us to our children and to future generations. The first chapter begins the moment the umbilical cord is cut and a new name is printed on a small birth certificate. The prints embedded on our hands and feet distinguish us from all others living on the planet. New chapters are continually added and the book of our life grows and will continue to be written until the angel of death closes our earthly book and we pass on to eternity.

I remember some of the early road I traveled, and I know the present path that I'm on. But I cannot see the ending, and I don't really care to know all of that. I just want to be ready for Christ's return or be prepared for my soul and spirit to leave my body at death, whichever comes first.

It seemed like the time was right to pen the memories of this journey for our friends, partners, and those who are just curious. In this book, I highlight the struggles, disappointments, attacks and victories, so that you will know what it is like being married to an evangelist with a global ministry. Those who know Perry well will tell you that he has always been completely open with people. You never have to wonder how he feels, what he is thinking, or what his opinion of a situation might be. He will tell you, and sometimes you don't even have to ask.

On the other hand, I am more guarded and will seldom express my thoughts and feelings to others, unless something is creating a negative impact. I can express myself better in writing than I ever could by standing before a crowd and speaking. After marrying Perry, there were times when I didn't feel qualified to be a minister's wife. However, Perry reminded me that he didn't need another preacher in the family. He didn't need a Gospel singer or a talented musician. He just wanted a wife, and that I could do.

People tend to view ministers through a different lens. Their perceptions are often formed by their denominational background or upbringing, which includes their own positive or negative experiences growing up in a particular church. I have heard some critics say that preachers need to get a 'real job.' Others comment that they wouldn't walk across the street to hear a certain preacher. But people who are converted to Christ or whose lives were changed by that same ministry often forge a lifelong connection or bond of friendship.

With Perry, it seems that people either like him or they don't. He says that a lot of people knew Jesus, Peter and Paul, and not everyone liked them, either. When Perry is slammed by critics, he reminds himself that he is in good company. People often mistreat those who are serving Christ. And sometimes, it is the Christians in the pews who are the worst—often because of their own past wounds that have never healed, or because of their denominational differences.

Many people have asked me what it is like living with someone who is not just another minister, but one whose name is known throughout the Christian world, and who is often recognized in restaurants, hotels, airports, and shopping malls. People ask me if he walks around praying all day, or if he sits in the living room and sees visions, or if he wakes me up speaking in tongues in the middle of the night. Others wonder if he lives at home what he lives in public. Does he have one personality for the ministry and another one for the family? Does he really love me and the kids the way he expresses, or is he saying that to impress others that he is a wonderful family man? In an age of hypocrisy and double standards, people want to know, "Am I supporting someone who is genuine, or someone who just sees the ministry as a business venture?"

All of these are legitimate questions. I can answer those questions because I have lived with him through good times and bad; I have seen both the admiration and the persecution he receives; and I know how he treats me and our children. I know the Perry that most people don't know.

For example, few outside of our ministry know that he gives the people who work for us at VOE or OCI a nickname, and even a ministry partner wouldn't know whom he's speaking of. There is Box, G.G, Mo-Si, The Greyhound Race Dog, Necee, Chuck E, Moner, Darlow, Android, and so on. He gives his family nicknames, too. I am Pammy Pooh, Amanda is Mander, and Jonathan is J.G. I have never asked him why he enjoys giving everybody a unique name, but with Perry he always finds some Scripture to back up what he does. Perhaps he read Revelation 3:12, "I will write on them a new name," and decided there is no point in waiting for heaven to get a name change. This is just one of his unique personality traits. Then there is his sense of humor, and his ability to study up to fourteen hours a day and enjoy it.

However, the real test for any minister is to walk the road of both worlds—one spiritual and invisible, and one natural and visible. In one world, he must deal with his wife, children, and office staff; but in the spiritual realm, he must have an ear to hear and deal with the spiritual problems and needs of multitudes of people. Perry is a man of God, and to Amanda, Jonathan and me, he is also Dad and husband. In the Christian world he is expected to be perfect; but to his family and friends, he can make mistakes and still be loved and accepted. To those who attend conferences and follow his ministry, he is expected to be serious; but to those who know him best, he is allowed to let his hair down, joke, exhibit flaws, and act like an overgrown kid. There has to be balance, and sometimes that is a challenge for Christians.

In this book, I will open the pages of my life so you can see this journey through my eyes. I will share my own life with you, and the life that comes with being married to a man who hears and sees in the spiritual world, and presents that message to a natural world. This is our story—sharing one life in two worlds.

Love and Prayers,
Pam Stone

PART ONE

IN THE BEGINNING

I ALMOST DIDN'T MAKE IT

HAVE YOU EVER heard a confession that shocked you? My mother, Stella, was visiting us in Cleveland when she told Perry and me a story that stunned us both.

First let me say that my parents had three children, all girls. Sheila is the oldest, Carla is the youngest, and I am in the middle. A few years ago, my mother told Perry and me that, before I was born, she and Dad were living in Chicago in an apartment while she was pregnant with me. Life was not easy in the city and Dad was working hard to make ends meet. With one child to feed and another on the way, Mom said she was feeling overwhelmed.

One day, while sitting in the kitchen, she was suddenly overcome with a thought that became very strong. A voice said to her, "Life is not worth living. You can end it all by jumping out the window and falling several stories below. It will be fast and quick. It will get you out of your misery." As she looked to the window, the thought became an image, and the image became a temptation to jump. Then she heard another voice say, "I gave life to you, and you need to give your baby a chance to live!"

The second voice that encouraged life began to overpower the first voice of death. While sitting at our dining room table telling this story,

Mom said, "I knew it was the voice of God telling me not to take my life because it would also take the life of my baby."

This was the first time I had ever heard this story. I had no idea that I almost didn't make it.

When you hear a story like this, it makes you wonder how things would have been different if my mother had not obeyed the right voice. What void would have been created if I—and then my younger sister Carla—had never been given the opportunity to live? At times we underestimate the significance of just one person's life—one person whose journey is interwoven with others, and eventually knitted together as a family.

The important thing is that my mother chose life, and the plan of God was not interrupted by premature death. Should there be someone reading this who is carrying an infant and becoming bombarded with negative thoughts that make you question whether you should give your child life, I want to say to you what the Lord said to my mother: "I gave life to you, and you need to give your baby a chance to live."

MY FAMILY BACKGROUND

On September 19, 1961, I entered the world at the Druid City Hospital in Tuscaloosa, Alabama and was named Pamela Jeannine Taylor. According to birth order studies, the middle child doesn't get much attention. My older sister, Sheila, had been accustomed to being the only child, so she demanded a lot of my mother's attention. Then my youngest sister, Carla, came along only nineteen months after I was born, so I had to learn to take care of myself. My mother said I was her most well-behaved baby. In four years, my mother gave birth to three girls.

We lived most of our lives around the area of Tuscaloosa, Alabama in the towns of Coker, Holt, or Cottondale. My family enjoyed camping in the summer, but the highlight of the year was definitely football season, between September and November. I grew up in a university town in the era of Paul "Bear" Bryant, longtime head coach of the University of Alabama's football team, so Saturdays were spent in front of the television with friends and family. I suppose that is why I like Alabama football to this day. To me it means family.

People often ask if my dad was a minister. They assume that, since Perry had several ministers in the family, then surely my dad must have been a minister, too. But that was not the case.

Throughout my childhood, neither of our parents went to church. To us, Sunday was just another day of the week. But thankfully, because of several relatives and friends of the family, my sisters and I were blessed to be able to attend church and hear the message of the Gospel of Christ.

Years ago, it was common for churches to have a bus ministry. Those who could afford it would drive through a neighborhood and go door to door, letting parents know that they would pick up their children for Sunday School and bring them back when the service ended. This was and still is a great ministry to reach children whose parents do not go to church, or who might not have transportation to bring them. When I was about twelve years old, my Aunt Gladys told my parents that she would pick us up in the church van for Sunday services.

We had gone to church with Aunt Gladys in the past. She took us to a Pentecostal church and I remember thinking the services were long. But we decided to give this particular church a try since we had nothing else to do on Sunday, anyway.

Aunt Gladys did what she could to plant the seeds in our heart for the Gospel to take root. Every child needs an Aunt Gladys. When we get to heaven, I believe she (and others like her) will be rewarded for their work. Aunt Gladys helped not only my family, but many others.

Each Sunday morning my two sisters and I would get dressed and wait at the front door for the van. We would arrive at the church and mingle with a large group of young people our age. I remember feeling loved by the people at the Northport Church of God and the youth group. Each Sunday and Wednesday, we looked forward to the church van picking us up so that we could attend church services.

This church was definitely different from the other churches we had visited, so we kept attending. At age thirteen, I joined the choir where my older sister was already singing. Eventually, all three of us joined the youth choir, where we sang during revivals, at the state camp meeting, and during the annual summer choir tour. This is where we made many memories and had so much fun with others our age.

Then the church decided to stop the van ministry. Our hearts were broken because there was nobody to take us to church. How would we get there? We had to go; church was our life, our lifeline, and our family.

My older sister Sheila had a learner's permit, which meant that she could drive a car if an adult rode in the front seat. We had no adult to place in the front seat, but our parents allowed her to drive us to church. This is how much we loved the church and desired to be in the services.

It was in this church that my sisters and I gave our lives to Christ, under the pastorate of Rev. Earl Hall. We prayed for our parents to be saved, and my mother was the first to give her life to Christ. Dad followed soon thereafter.

This was the most joyous time of my childhood because we served God as a family. But the euphoria didn't last long. Mother decided she wasn't going to church anymore and Daddy also stopped going because he didn't want to answer the question when people asked, "Where is your wife?"

When I asked my mother years later why she stopped attending church, she said that she couldn't forgive Dad for all the things he had done in the past. She couldn't understand why all the church folks thought he was such a good man when they didn't know what the past had been like. After my parents stopped attending church, problems developed and soon grew until the word "divorce" crept in. When I was fourteen, our parents divorced. It's sad to see that unforgiveness was the plot of the enemy that destroyed my family.

The people in the church had become our family. One family that was particularly special to us was Jerry and Charlotte Skelton and their two boys, Jarrod and Terrill, whom I babysat for. I was close friends with Charlotte's sister, Tanya Talley, and spent many weekends at her house.

The Skelton's knew how unhappy we were at home after the divorce, and they opened their hearts and home to all three of us girls. It still amazes me that a family would open their home and allow three girls to move in with them. They were the epitome of the love of Christ in action. They treated us no differently from their own children. Even on Christmas and birthdays, we were all treated the same. I had to have surgery while I lived with them, and I did not have insurance. I never heard any discussion about how they would pay for this; they just paid it.

One advantage to Charlotte was that she now had three live-in babysitters and house cleaners. She taught us how to cook. When Perry and I were married, they were the "parents" of the bride. They even paid for the wedding, and Jerry walked me down the aisle and gave me away to my prince charming.

Charlotte's family had a singing group called The Talley Family. They traveled around and sang at churches, revivals, and conventions. In February of 1980 they booked a service at a church in Selma, Alabama. I had my eye on the drummer of the group, so I decided to go along for the ride. In the service that night, we met a young man who told us he was coming to our church for a revival in a few weeks. His name was Perry Fred Stone, Jr.

He did come to our church; and during that four-week revival, after the Friday night services the youth group came to the Skelton home where they sang, prayed, and fellowshipped. During this time I learned more about this dark-haired evangelist from Virginia. I loved God in him before I loved him.

It is not easy to see your parents go through a divorce and have your family break apart. But God took something bad and turned it into something good. What if I hadn't been close to the Talley's and had not gone to Selma and met Perry for the first time? What if I had not been living in the Skelton home and had not had the times of fellowship and the phone calls after the revival? All of these things led up to a relationship with him, until finally we married on April 2, 1982. I will be forever grateful to Jerry and Charlotte Skelton for the role they played in my life. They helped me become the person I am today.

PERRY'S FAMILY BACKGROUND

Perry had a much different family background than I did. There are four generations of ministers in his family, not including his Uncle Rufus whom you've heard him talk about. In his book, *Fire on the Altar*, Perry's dad, Fred Stone, wrote about Rufus and his spiritual influence on the Dunford and Stone families.

Perry's dad was a minister before Perry was born. Fred was converted to Christ during a great "coal field revival" in West Virginia in the late 1940s. Shortly thereafter, Fred began to evangelize in West Virginia and Kentucky, often hitchhiking from revival to revival. About three years after he and Juanita married, Fred began to pastor small churches in West Virginia, then Maryland, and later Virginia— the state where Perry began his evangelistic ministry. Perry has great memories of his life during that time, where his dad pastored in Big Stone Gap, Arlington, and Salem.

He had wonderful grandparents on both sides of the family (even though he was, as his mom says, often mischievous). The family got together at certain times of the year, generally Christmas or summertime, and many memories were made during these visits. The small town of Davis, West Virginia where his mom's parents lived was a winter wonderland as over a foot of snow would often blanket the ground and trees during the Christmas season.

When Perry was young, he loved comedy. The family watched The Smother's Brothers on television, and his Granddad Bava never missed a Hee Haw program. Granddad Bava was a jovial man who was nearly always laughing or telling somebody a joke. His humor remained for as long as he was conscious, as the day he was headed for surgery, he was on the gurney, telling one last joke and making everyone smile.

This same humor was evident on Perry by age eleven when he had memorized Flip Wilson's records and could repeat his jokes word for word. He also would play jokes on people with odd items he bought— a fly in a plastic ice cube, gum that caused your mouth to pucker, a hand buzzer, or a cushion that made a certain noise when someone sat on it. While Perry is introverted in many ways, he still has the ability to be funny or to be a jokester. He can also imitate people's voices.

He sometimes roams though the offices at VOE changing his voice to mimic some well-known minister, causing the staff to say, "There he goes again, entertaining himself." Comedy is one of his methods of stress relief, and our son Jonathan has the same gift.

Granddad Bava, Juanita's dad, once had a radio program, and during those years, he used to tape almost everything. If he didn't have it on audio reel-to-reel, he had it on video. It must run in the family, because Granddad's sister Millie always has a camera in her hand and is ready to capture a moment, whether you are ready for a picture or not.

Many of Granddad Bava's reel-to-reel tapes have been transferred to newer technology, so we still have the ability to watch or listen to something he recorded. He recorded church services, and he has the grandchildren on tape, either singing, reading, or telling jokes. One of those tapes is dated June 1959, which was the year that Granddad started the Gorman Church of God. That was the same month Perry was born, and the Gorman church was the church where he preached his first revival. On tape are Perry's great-grandfather Pete Bava, his grandfather John Bava, and his father, Fred Stone.

Perry's most significant memories were made when his father pastored churches in Arlington and Salem. Each year in Virginia, the denomination hosted youth camps at the state campground in Roanoke. Perry attended the camps each year, from ages eleven to nineteen, and served in his late teens as a dormitory room counselor. At age eleven, on a Thursday night at youth camp, he received the infilling of the Holy Spirit, which would prove to be a pivotal encounter with God for his later call into the ministry. At age sixteen, he joined with three friends during a late Sunday night prayer meeting, and that is when Perry was called into the ministry.

When Perry began his full-time evangelistic ministry at age eighteen, someone would often take pictures during the services. Today at the VOE office, there is a cabinet that holds thousands of pictures that captured the revivals, camp meetings, conferences, and mission trips. Perry can look at a picture and remember where it was taken and the results of the meeting. He says that a picture captures a moment in time that makes a memory.

Today, with digital cameras, cell phones and iPads, it is easier to capture a moment. Our daughter has thousands of photographs and takes pictures every chance she gets. The picture taking DNA has been passed on! It is good to make memories and record them for future generations to enjoy. People who had a wonderful family background will always enjoy going back and reflecting upon those memories. A cabinet in our home is packed with photo albums that date back to the time of our marriage.

God forms a path for each person to follow—a road traveled by faith that leads to an unknown future. If you wait for God's will, your path will eventually cross the path of the person God has chosen to be your husband or wife. Once the covenant is sealed, your paths join as one on the road of destiny. This is what happened when Perry conducted a four-week revival at my home church in Northport, Alabama in 1980.

CHAPTER 2

THE EARLY YEARS

I T WAS A cold Sunday morning in February of 1980 when a twenty-year-old single evangelist named Perry Stone came to our home church in Northport, Alabama to conduct a revival. The meeting was scheduled for one week, but crowds filled the building and the spiritual results caused the church to ask him to continue for a second week. At the end of the second week, Perry strongly felt it should continue a third week, but he had another revival scheduled that week.

On Saturday morning he called the pastor of the church in Sylacauga, Alabama where he was to begin the next revival. The pastor said, "You cannot cancel this revival at my church. It is planned and already advertised." Perry agreed to close the Northport revival after two weeks and get up early Sunday morning and drive to Sylacauga. But on Saturday night around 9:30, in the middle of a prayer line, the Lord jolted Perry and said, "Did I tell you to leave here?"

"No, you did not," he replied. He stopped the prayer line and said to the people, "I'll be back in a minute." He went into the main office and called the Sylacauga pastor to tell him, "I'm sorry, but for some reason I cannot come. God's will is for me to be here." The pastor was understandably upset. Perry returned and announced, "The revival is going on."

In that third week, while standing on the platform praying during a service, the Lord clearly spoke to Perry as he looked in my direction and said, "That is the girl you are going to marry." He immediately began to rebuke this mental stronghold, only to hear the voice repeat, "I said that is the girl you are going to marry." The word went from his head into his spirit, and he jokes that he prayed with one eye closed and the other open, watching me. He was watching and praying.

When Perry arrived at Northport, he was engaged to a girl in Virginia, but he was strongly sensing that it was not the will of God. During the second week of the revival, the girl called him and broke up with him. So when the Lord spoke to him, he was not looking for a wife, so he did not expect to hear such a word.

At that time I had dated two different young men in the church, which was more of a friendship than a serious relationship. However, if Perry had not heard and obeyed the Lord that Saturday and had gone to the next revival, he and I might not have connected; and had we not, we would have missed the *perfect* will of God. In life, what appears at times to be a *little* decision may actually be a *destiny* decision. Two years later the will of God was sealed when we covenanted our lives with marriage vows.

I graduated from high school in 1979 and, while in school, I also worked for the Skelton family and helped do housework and care for their children. Right after high school, I applied for a secretarial position at the University of Alabama. I assumed I would graduate from high school and live in Tuscaloosa for the rest of my life. But not long after the revival in 1980, Perry began to contact me by phone and letters. I told the Lord, "If I'm going to stay and live in this city, then let me get a job. If I'm going to live somewhere else, then pass me up for the job opportunity."

I interviewed for the job and things looked promising. But I didn't get that job and never applied for another one. I chose to continue working for the Skelton family. The Lord knew more than I could perceive, and He was aligning events to bring forth my destiny.

I've always believed that we go through things for a reason. We might not always see the reason at the time; but if we put our faith and trust in God, we will find our way. Working at the Skelton's offered several advantages over a traditional job; one being that after Perry and I started dating, this allowed me to spend more time with him when he came to town, and even allowed me to make a couple of visits to see his family, who were living in Salem, Virginia then.

In a way, my parents' divorce even worked to my advantage. Many young women marry and are attached to their parents and siblings; yet they find that they must, reluctantly, move far away from home and their familiar roots. Since I was not living at home, and since my parents were divorced, the idea of traveling was appealing to me. I would see my mom and sisters when I could, which was about twice a year, and the remaining time I would travel with Perry once we were married.

On one occasion, a few months before we married, Perry asked me to drive with him from Northport to Cleveland, Tennessee because he needed to take a book manuscript to a printer. I agreed, and we set off early that morning. I thought along the way that we might stop somewhere and eat. But not Perry! The trip took about four hours, and we arrived at the printer where he introduced me and then sat down to give instructions for the job. As we were getting on the interstate to drive back to Tuscaloosa, he finally looked at me and said, "Hey, do you need something to eat? We could stop by McDonald's." In those days Perry fasted continually. He would say, "Food and the Holy Spirit don't get along." In those days, when you traveled with him on the road, he seldom stopped for anything except fuel.

I think he assumed that since he fasted so much, maybe I should, too. But I wasn't accustomed to his fasting lifestyle. He got me something to eat at McDonalds on the drive back to Northport, and of course we had to opt for the drive-through since there was no time to waste in a restaurant for a sit-down meal.

Courting has its disadvantages and marriage its advantages. When you are dating, you might not speak up. But after being married a few years, you can move from saying nothing to barking a few orders like, "I'm hungry. Stop at the next exit so I can eat."

In the two years that Perry and I "dated", we went on a real date only one time. This was because of his travel schedule, and the fact that he would briefly pass through town and then would be on the road again. Our one official date was at the Western Steer Steak House about forty-five minutes away in Birmingham. We ate dinner, held hands, talked for two hours, and returned to Northport. The rest of the time we were with friends, family, or other young people in a home or church setting. He and I stayed in touch by phone.

This was before the days of cell phones and discount plans, so you paid for every minute you talked. The month before he asked me to marry him Perry's phone bill was five hundred dollars. This motivated him to propose to me, since he thought it would cost less to be married than to maintain a long distance relationship by phone.

THOSE UGLY TIES

Before we married, Perry's family moved from Salem, Virginia to Wildwood, Florida to pastor a church. The town of Wildwood is near Ocala, and much of Perry's traveling itinerary at the time was Virginia, Alabama, Georgia and Tennessee. Moving to Florida would have been inconvenient for him, so he moved to my home town and rented an apartment from a member of our church.

The day he moved in, several of us came to help him move boxes and unpack. He didn't own much, but he did have the most horrible collection of ties you can imagine. As I pulled ties by the dozens from a box, they ranged from ugly to hideous. I discovered that Perry was a connoisseur of bizarre looking ties, like a chef who experiments with strange foods. But a chief on a bad day was better than Perry's ties on a good day.

What is an ugly tie? How about a purple tie with white polka dots? Or a dark purple tie with large white circles that played tricks on your eyes if you looked at it long enough. Or a tie covered with elephants. Now, I'm fond of elephants because the Big Al mascot for the University of Alabama's football team wears an elephant costume. But did somebody with the Republican Party give him this tie? Imagine Perry in a black suit, wearing a hideous tie, and preaching a message on having a sound mind.

We were engaged to be married at the time, but it looked as though the ties that bind might become the ties that separate. I pulled out another tie that had buildings imprinted on it. I cast that one into the box of outer darkness, never to be seen again. I wasn't even sure if I should donate these rejects to a thrift store.

Pulling the dozens of ties from the box and separating them into accept and reject piles almost got me thrown out of the apartment. Every time I said, "This tie must go," Perry would grab it like a kid ready to have his favorite toy put in a yard sale and say, "But my friend in Elliston, Virginia gave me that tie for my birthday!"

Each tie held a special memory and had its own story. He knew the place, the occasion, and the revival. These ties were like lifelong friends who had stood with him through good and the bad. I don't know if his friends were color blind, or if they gave him these ties as a joke, or if they just had bad taste. That's when I realized that Perry really didn't care what he looked like behind the pulpit, as long as it was a suit and a tie. And any tie would do. He might have been the world's worst-dressed preacher, but he knew the story behind every tie.

I came to the last tie. Without asking permission, I carried the box to a car so the ugly ties could be donated to a thrift store. I lived in the area another year before we married, and I don't know if they ever sold those ties. I never saw anyone in town sporting one of them.

His shoes were another issue. Perry had picked up a habit from his dad. Fred was thrifty, practical, and always neatly dressed, but he never paid retail for anything. He liked to visit second-hand stores and yard sales, and his shoes came from a certain discount store. They looked great on the outside, and they held up if they weren't worn often. Perry wore the same discount shoes. But Perry preached almost every night and he paced back and forth the entire time he preached. It was like watching a tennis match. He got such a workout that his shoes wore out quickly and he wore holes in the soles. In his earlier ministry, every pair of shoes had holes in them. He was teased for preaching the leather off his shoes.

On one occasion he split the back of one shoe and used black electrical tape to hold it together. He never shopped because he didn't have time. But he didn't care that his shoe was held together by electrical tape, because he figured the back of his pants would cover it.

Those were the shoes he wore to preach at the most prestigious church in our denomination—the North Cleveland Church of God. In this church were business leaders, Lee College and seminary professors, academic administrators, and others who were well-known in the community. There was Perry, leaping across the stage and flashing those taped shoes to the audience and the choir.

Pastor Joe Edwards told the church, "This single evangelist needs some help. He has electrical tape holding his shoe together. He either needs a wife or a new pair of shoes."

A precious elderly woman who was a member of the church recognized that, while this young man could preach, he was clueless about the proper way to dress.

After the pastor's announcement, the next day Perry found a box under the pulpit that contained a brand new pair of black Florsheim shoes, accompanied by flowers and a note welcoming him to the church. He slipped on those new shoes, and from that moment on, he never bought another pair of shoes at the discount store. He concluded it was better to pay a few more dollars to have comfortable shoes that would last longer, since he wore out shoes like a NASCAR driver wears out tires.

I knew I had an assignment to try to help him dress better and match his clothes. That has been more of a challenge than you might think. He wanted to wear whatever he wanted to wear, whenever he wanted to wear it. He could not match colors. He never owned a pair of jeans until he was in his 40s. When he was younger, everybody wore them, but he stuck with polyester black pants and five suits. Now he wants to be comfortable, so typically, he wears jeans and seldom is seen wearing a tie.

When he was single he didn't think about dry cleaning his suits, which can be a problem when you perspire in the same five suits for weeks and weeks. Eventually someone in the church would say, "Do you need your suits dry cleaned?" Birdie Viars, a lady from Pulaski, Virginia was in Perry's five-week revival and years later said, "He wore the same black suit every night and I could see that jacket standing up in the corner without a coat hanger. So I took his suits to the cleaners."

It was obvious that his emphasis was not on outward appearance. I guess he figured that if John the Baptist would wear camel hair and a leather girdle, he could wear whatever works. Black was his favorite color suit. But at one time he had sports jackets in the colors of red, yellow, green, and purple. He preached in them. I finally convinced him during a Holy Land tour to leave those jackets for the poor people in Israel. A year later I saw a young Arab boy wearing that bright green jacket on the Mount of Olives.

I couldn't even leave wedding attire up to him. Here is a letter dated February 2, 1982 from Perry's mother, as we were planning the wedding:

> Dear Pam,
>
> It's me again! I got the sample of material. I'll try to get Melanie's dress here. Diana hopes to be in the wedding. I talked to her the other night. Since Phil is going to be an usher, what are they going to wear? Perry told Phil they would just wear black suits. He is kidding, isn't he? Does he mean a black tux? He also said he would just wear a black suit. Please tell me he doesn't mean that, too."

So, I had to start shopping for him, and I tried to redress him after marriage. I made him stop wearing a white belt that he wore with his black suit. I chose ties and made sure things matched. When he began airing Manna-fest from Israel, he wore jogging outfits because he reasoned they were lighter to pack, less likely to wrinkle, and were colorful for the camera. But the ministry began to receive phone calls from viewers asking, "Who in the world dresses him? Can you get someone else to do it?" He has been known to send a VOE employee to a store in town that sold "seconds merchandise" to pick up some sweaters for him to wear on the Manna-fest telecast.

Today I don't say much about how he dresses, because our children and the college-aged young people tell him when something doesn't match, doesn't look good, or is out of style. Being connected with the younger generation does have its advantages. Our daughter Amanda is especially hard on her dad when it comes to his clothes. She wastes no time telling him if he is not looking as he should. When she gets that look on her face and starts laughing, he goes back to the closet and changes.

This brings me to the one of many reasons God places a wife in a man's life. Men tend to enjoy sports and the outdoors, and they might come home filthy and smelling like a sardine. But a good wife will see beyond the fisherman and bring balance to her man in many areas, if he will listen to her and not reject her advice.

WARNED IN ADVANCE

Before a couple weds, they spend months getting to know each other through dating. Many of the young people in our youth ministry, including girls in their twenties, will go out to eat or to an event with a group, but they will not date. They believe the dating game often creates emotional ties that will be severed if things don't work out with the young man.

Godly men and women are progressively formed by the hand of the potter into vessels of honor. It happens over time. If you don't like his or her ways today, know that those faults will only increase after marriage. Once the man catches his dear, the hunt is over and he has little motivation to change his ways.

When I married Perry, he was almost twenty-three years old and was already established as an evangelist. His revivals often lasted weeks. Before we were married, Perry preached a seven-week revival, followed by a three-week revival in Montgomery, Alabama. We married and went straight to a three-week revival in Gastonia, North Carolina, which Pastor Walter Mauldin (who was one of my former pastors at Northport) jokingly called, "the honeymoon revival."

I was marrying a young man who had lived alone, traveled alone, prayed alone, and stayed alone in a hotel room or a bedroom of a pastor's home. He had a lone ranger lifestyle for five years. Suddenly, another person was going to live with him, travel with him, and be around him twenty-four hours a day. For most young men, that might have been an exciting new journey.

However, Perry's daily routine was so established—six hours of study, between two and three hours of prayer, a three hour or longer church service, and repeat the process the next day—that he was sincerely afraid that marriage would hinder his focus.

He had already cultivated a comfortable habit that he could not break, even after marriage. We were married on Friday evening, drove to the Red Lobster to eat with the family and friends, spent the night at the Holiday Inn, and got up the next day and drove to North Carolina to begin a twenty-one day revival. Postponing the revival for a few days never occurred to him.

A few days before our wedding, we were in the home of the family I lived with, and Perry said he needed to have a serious discussion with me. I couldn't imagine what this discussion would be, because I thought we had covered everything already. We were alone at the kitchen table and Perry said, "Look, I want to make this clear. I spend a lot of time in prayer and Bible study, and I cannot allow myself to be distracted during the day." I already knew this.

But the next statement was odd, and we both look back and laugh about it. He told me, "I refuse to be married to someone who is going to nag and complain. Now you definitely are not that way. But if you turn into a biddy and start driving me crazy with nagging and complaints, I'll go on a forty-day fast and ask God to take you on."

He seemed to be serious so I decided not to laugh. I simply replied, "Oh, ok." We were laughing about this recently and he asked me, "What were you really thinking when I said that to you?" I replied, "I was thinking, 'the same goes for you buster.'"

Perry's routine has been set since he was eighteen and it hasn't changed much. For years he never ate breakfast. He only began doing so when he was diagnosed with diabetes in his late 40s. For many years he would eat only one meal a day, but now he realizes he needs to take better care of himself.

When he was eighteen, he preached outside of Princeton, West Virginia at the Montcalm Church of God where Polly and Gilbert Blair pastored. Several years ago in Beckley, Polly was present at a church that was honoring Perry and his dad for their ministries. She stood and told of how her church hosted one of Perry's first long revivals. She added, "My husband and I cannot recall Perry ever coming out of the bedroom during the day to eat. He stayed in the room, studying and praying all day long."

I believe it was this intense dedication, love for God and the Word, and the lifestyle of fasting and praying that God observed when He kept his eye on Perry through his teen years and into his twenties. The blessings and favor we experience today are a result of many years of sacrifice, fasting, and prayers that were planted in the early days.

As years have passed, there have been more responsibilities related to the ministry. But Perry is still just as focused on studying, writing, and sermon preparation, and he still has the same fire burning in his spirit that he felt the night he heard the Lord say, "I have called you to preach." And I have the same love for him that I had when I told Charlotte Skelton in Northport, Alabama, "I love him."

CHAPTER 3

WANTED:
A PREACHER

TIME HAS CHANGED things as it relates to the kind of man most Christian women want to marry. Today, most are looking for the man who has financial stability and can provide security and a comfortable lifestyle. In my day, a single Christian girl who dreamed about her future husband often wanted to marry someone who was in the ministry. Options were limited, though, because there were not many single ministers to choose from.

Sometimes that dream was not her own; instead, it was planted by her mother or grandmother who had high hopes that their daughter or granddaughter would marry a minister and work in the kingdom of God. Marrying a minister was a road that instantly led to a life-long journey in the church. These mothers and grandmothers spent a lot of time in prayer the moment they discovered that a young, single preacher was coming to the church to serve on staff or preach a revival.

In the late 1970s, several young, single preachers came to the Northport Church of God for revivals. The longer the revival, the more hope the adults had that the Lord would answer their prayer, and their daughter or granddaughter would be chosen by that minister to eventually become his wife.

I recall four evangelists, all unmarried, who preached revivals at our church. Three were Wayne Graves, Freddie Edwards, and Marcus

Lamb—the same Marcus Lamb who founded Daystar Television Network. Marcus preached in a white suit with a red carnation on Easter, and with his strong Georgia accent, he could imitate the television minister Earnest Angley. The fourth minister came to our church in February of 1980. He was skinny with a headful of thick black hair and a pale complexion, as though he never saw the sun. He was from Virginia and his revivals were lasting for weeks. That was about all we knew.

When he arrived and started preaching, people noticed that he had a lot of spiritual knowledge and was an anointed speaker. He was also interesting to listen to and the young people enjoyed his sermons. The first Sunday morning of the revival, two young men came back to the Lord, and both would later enter the ministry. Many young people, and even entire families, accepted Christ or rededicated their lives during this revival.

There were a few single girls among our seventy-member youth group who thought they could be chosen to become Mrs. Stone. They talked about what it must be like to be married to a minister who traveled. A few wanted to marry a minister, but I was not one of them.

In time I wanted to be married to a good husband and a man of God. But at no time did I imagine or even pray that the Lord would send me a minister. I never felt like preacher's wife material. I was not a piano player, which was almost a requirement for a pastor's wife in those days. And while I could sing, I was nervous and uncomfortable in front of people. I also didn't have the right kind of family background. I felt I had a lot to offer as a wife, but not as a minister's wife.

You know the rest of the story. I was the very one the Lord chose to be his wife. When the revival ended and Perry left in his white Buick, I knew I had fallen in love—not with a ministry, but with a young man. When he came to our church, the youth were starting to scatter, and the four weeks he spent with us became a turning point for all of us. During that revival, Perry saw a vision one day of me sitting in a chair and praying to receive the baptism of the Holy Spirit. That night he brought out a chair and sat it in the front for me to sit in. Over an hour later, after praying in the corner of the church, I received the baptism of the Holy Spirit. I was also baptized in water. So I loved Perry's obedience to God and the way he allowed God to use him.

Prior to his departure from Northport, he asked for phone numbers to stay in contact with his new friends. He also asked for the phone number of the couple I was living with at the time, Charlotte and Jerry Skelton. After Perry left I told Charlotte, "I am in love with him." Charlotte replied, "Well, he is on his way to another revival, so don't get your hopes up. He'll probably meet another girl in the next revival."

When he arrived back in Virginia, he started calling the house and I would answer the phone. Then I started receiving letters from him—letters that I still have to this day. After several months of calls and letters, he paid a surprise visit to Charlotte and Jerry's house. That evening when we were together talking, he whispered in my ear, "I'm in love with you." At that moment I knew the deal was sealed. I would one day become his wife and build a life with him.

God has a sense of humor, because I was such an unlikely candidate to marry a minister—especially one who would eventually have a ministry impacting over 250 nations of the world. I had not been in church from birth, my parents were divorced, I have no formal academic training, and my first and only job was babysitting young children, cleaning, and cooking dinner. Had I known where the ministry was headed, I might have had an inferiority complex and said to the Lord, "I'm not what Perry and this ministry need." My confidence could not be in my ability or personality, but in the call and plan of God.

The wife of any minister must also be called by the Lord to the ministry of her husband. Some women choose to marry a minister, and others are called to be a minister's wife. If a woman decides without God's approval to marry a man who is involved in ministry, her commitment might waiver if circumstances became negative. We have known of ministers' wives who left their husbands because the ministry was not what they thought it would be. The perception of a glamorous life turned into reality and she couldn't handle it. A woman who is called will stand by her husband through good and bad. She will be a true helpmate, because she carries the same call that her husband carries.

Those whom God calls, He equips. My equipping would come from the weeks, months and years of traveling on the road and learning to manage an office before we had employees. You pull from the inner strength and God-given abilities that emerge in different situations. We grow in both the grace and the knowledge of God. Knowledge reveals God's will, but grace gives us the ability to perform God's will.

ATTRACTED TO THE PREACHER

In any church congregation are Christian women who are married to an unsaved husband who is not the spiritual priest of the family. For some women who deal with a difficult husband, it can become a mental stronghold if she starts imagining what it would be like to be married to a minister. I am not speaking of a physical relationship fantasy or lust of the flesh. I am speaking of the woman imagining what it would be like to have a husband who loves God that much, who prays, and who doesn't rebuke her for attending church or giving offerings. The woman might observe that a minister is always well-dressed, always smiling and shaking hands, and always speaking kind and encouraging remarks. The woman thinks to herself, "Why not me, Lord? Why was I left out of this scenario?"

One of the reasons some women look at a minister this way might have nothing to do with his looks or his smile. It might have more to do with the anointing he carries. The anointing can turn an average minister who is just a regular guy into another man, as it did with King Saul. The Bible says, "Then the Spirit of the Lord will come upon you, and you will prophesy with them and be turned into another man" (1 Sam. 10:6).

When the anointing is released, there are increased feelings of faith, joy, mercy, compassion and love. There is a spiritual intimacy created between that person and God, when the power of the Holy Spirit is flowing in the church service. The anointing and ministry of the Word, accompanied with spiritual authority, is a magnetic force that unites believers and causes the entire church to bond together. Often, it is the anointing that people are pulled toward, as the presence of God brings positive emotions and peace, which so many people are lacking in their private lives.

The openness and love that the presence of the Lord brings means that individuals must guard their own fleshly emotions so they are not mixed with the spiritual ones. A spiritual love is pure, but a carnal love can conceal lust. Since the Holy Spirit must open the door of a person's heart to spiritual intimacy with God, once the heart is open, it is also open to love brothers and sisters in Christ.

Occasionally we hear stories of a man and woman in a church, and both were married to other people, but both became involved romantically with one another. Sometimes this started when they talked following a service. Once an affair started, it didn't make sense that this could happen after people had been in the presence of the Lord.

The best way to explain this mystery came from Dr. Jerry Milili, a pastor and medical doctor from Baton Rouge, Louisiana. Years ago, Perry preached at his church. During one visit he explained how that, years ago in the church youth camps, the leaders began to observe something troubling and unexplainable. After some of the greatest and most anointed youth camp services, where teenaged boys and girls spent hours in the word and prayer, there would be a tendency for some of them to sneak away from adult supervision and make out somewhere on the campground. On a few occasions, a girl became pregnant.

In a meeting to discuss how to deal with this problem the question arose, "Why does this happen after such powerful services?"

Dr. Milili told Perry that, after looking into the situation, they concluded the following. When the presence of God would fill the auditorium for hours, it created an intimacy between the worshipper and God. This intimacy would fill the heart and spirit with feelings of peace, joy and love. These young people, especially the girls, had their hearts opened and were sensing the perfect love of God. As they left the service each night, there were some whose emotions were open to receiving any form of love and affection. The enemy, using the charged emotions of young people, took advantage of the situation, as the girl's heart was open to intimacy. Lust is the enemy's attempt to pervert the love of God that comes from being in His presence. This is not an excuse for such actions, but perhaps it is an explanation.

While some in the church may move off the straight and narrow path and begin to walk the road of carnality, the reality is that people cannot accomplish their God-given assignments without the power and self-control that comes through the Holy Spirit.

PART TWO

LIFE AFTER MARRIAGE

CHAPTER 4

LIFE IN CLEVELAND, TENNESSEE

A FTER OUR FRIDAY night marriage and the twenty-one day "honeymoon revival" in Gastonia, North Carolina, we went home to an apartment in Cleveland. The apartment was owned by Dale and Brenda Hughes, a family who would later become friends of ours. Their son Richie had been a star quarterback in one of the high schools and had received the Holy Spirit baptism during Perry's revival.

Our second story apartment was perfect for the average newly married couple, but there was nothing average about us for several reasons. Most newlyweds unpack furniture, clothes, kitchen utensils, and so on. But our belongings consisted of books stacked in boxes, hundreds of blank cassette tapes, boxes of cassette tape labels, revival packets, advertisements, and tape duplicators. This filled up one bedroom.

We were receiving a small number of orders and many invitations to minister, so I asked my sister Sheila to move to Cleveland and live in our apartment since we were on the road most of the time. We gave her our bedroom, which was the only one remaining in the apartment. Sheila kept up with the mail and filled orders while we were away. When we came home for a few days, we removed the cushions from the living room couch and slept on them on the floor. When you are young and newly married, that is not as bad as it might seem.

Before long, more boxes of books and resource materials overtook the living space in the apartment, and that sent us looking for a house. We purchased a split-level house with two upstairs bedrooms and a nice basement that would provide much-needed office space. Perry worked for hours in that basement. After Jonathan was born, I would put him in a baby carrier and work right beside Perry when we were home. We knew some young people from the area who would visit occasionally. Before they left, Perry would have them downstairs typing labels, duplicating messages, and helping to pack for the next revival.

Every few months, Perry wrote and self-published sermon booklets. He would have these printed, storing more boxes in the house and taking up needed living space. Closets and even the kitchen were filling up with ministry material. Having an office in your home is convenient but we decided we should move the office outside our home for two reasons. First, we didn't have the space anymore. And second, having an office at home means you work constantly, so it distracts from family time. Moving the office would give us needed space and help us separate work time from family time.

We rented a 350-square-foot office. Many times Perry and someone who was helping him would come from work and ask, "What's for dinner?" You could get almost any young man from the local college to volunteer his time if you promised him a home-cooked meal.

In the early phases of the ministry, our income was so limited that we could not hire full-time employees to help while we were on the road. Our first employee was Monty Franklin, a pastor's son from Alabama. He was a student at Lee College (now Lee University) who volunteered much of his time until we were able to pay him a few dollars an hour. I tried to make it up to him by cooking dinner for him when we were in town. Several other young men from Lee College helped from time to time, including Victor Bacon, Carey Lawhon, and others.

Before long we moved from that tiny office to a 2,000-square-foot office on Broad Street, about one block from the ministry offices of Norvel Hayes, a well-known teacher in Charismatic circles. The building was being sold for $95,000, which was money we did not have. But the Lord helped us obtain this office, which we used for over four years. A man from Virginia moved his family to Cleveland to become our office manager. That lasted about a year, because we were not able to pay him the money he needed to meet his family obligations.

Prior to this person stepping down, we were ministering in Anniston, Alabama when suddenly the Holy Spirit directed Perry to call out seven young men and give each one a word from the Lord for their life or some particular situation they were encountering. Among the seven was a 21-year-old named Charlie Ellis, who often traveled to the revivals on week-ends. The anointing came over Perry and he pointed his finger at Charlie and said, "You will one day work with me in Cleveland."

After accepting the resignation of our one full-time employee, Perry immediately called Charlie and offered him the job. Being single and having no family obligations, he was there within two weeks and has been with us since 1989. Later Perry's brother, Phillip, assisted us part-time. Throughout the ministry, the Lord always had the right people in place to hire as the need arose.

Almost every revival continued nightly for two to four weeks, and we found ourselves closing one revival and heading to another. When we returned home, we had only a few days to catch up on things. Sometimes Charlie and Perry worked eighteen-hour days, often not taking time to eat. Charlie is still as hard-working and dedicated as he was the day he first arrived.

A few years passed and we outgrew this office and needed a larger facility. We drove around Cleveland searching for any building for sale and could find nothing. Eventually we spoke to a restaurant owner who was planning to relocate, and he offered to sell us his 7,500 square-foot brick building. This was one of the few times we ever borrowed money for a ministry project because we were under a deadline on the option to buy. The bank loan was approved thirty minutes before we would have lost the option.

After the purchase, our dear friends Russell and Dorothy Spaulding of WBPI TV-49 and Watchmen Broadcasting, spent several weeks constructing our first studio set, many years before the Manna-fest telecast. The studio was used to tape prophetic videos that would be offered on

Christian telethons and in the revival services. The only challenge was that the ceiling was so low that Perry had to sit in a chair to teach. You can imagine how difficult this was for somebody who can hardly speak without pacing back and forth.

The ministry hit a growth period after this, and we were able to hire several more staff personnel. Bill Cloud came on board to assist Perry with writing and research. We hired people to handle phone calls and orders. During this time, Perry's parents moved to Cleveland and his mother, Juanita, was hired on staff. She still works in the office and has assisted Perry in his ministry for about thirty-five years.

Eventually we outgrew this office, too, and we both felt it was time to find property and build. Around 1996 we located about fourteen acres for sale with an asking price of $220,000. When the family learned that a ministry wanted to buy it, they decided to sell it for $180,000. We learned that their mother was a devoted Baptist with a heart for world missions. She would sit on the porch of her home and pray, overlooking the field where our offices are now sitting. She prayed for souls to be won into God's Kingdom, especially on the mission field. So this property was prophetically significant, in more ways than one.

Back in 1988 in Leeds, Alabama, during the third week of a four-week tent revival in the month of July, God gave Perry a clear vision of a gentleman in a black suit telling him that God was going to give him a television ministry if he would preach what God told him and go when and where God directed him. A third instruction was so personal that, to this day, Perry has never revealed the information, either publicly or to me.

After this vision, Perry drew what he saw on paper, including a set of concrete steps, an old road, and the type of land he saw in this vision. The property we purchased from this family to build the Voice of Evangelism offices had the exact concrete steps, the old road, and the property layout that he saw in the 1988 vision. This is why we knew this was the right location.

The first building, which was a 25,000 square-foot office, was paid for on the day of the building dedication. The second phase, a 45,000 square-foot studio and office building, was paid for about two months before the building was open and dedicated. The third phase, which was just completed, is the OCI Gathering Place. This beautiful facility was paid for through God's miraculous provision about five months before the day the building was dedicated during the July 2013 Partner's Homecoming.

ON THE ROAD

Throughout the 1980s and early 1990s, we typically stayed in the pastor's home or parsonage throughout the entire revival. Some ministers had children living at home, while others were older and had no family living with them. Those people enjoyed the company. Typically, my mornings were spent typing labels and running cassette tapes of the services, assisting the pastor's wife with chores, or helping her fix a late lunch since Perry didn't eat until after two o'clock p.m.

When returning home after service—usually ten o'clock or later—Perry and the pastor would often watch the news. But instead of going to bed, Perry would stay up and study more, often falling sleep about two o'clock a.m. or later. I have never had his energy, mental motivation, or drive. Still today, he works like a multi-tasker on steroids. He will watch the news, type a message, listen to a CD, be on the Internet or a second computer, and talk to somebody sitting across from his desk, while texting someone a message.

The first year I traveled with Perry, I would kneel beside him and pray. This is embarrassing to admit, but sometimes I would be so exhausted that I would fall asleep. The moment he noticed that I was asleep, he would yell, "Glory to God," so loud that it would jar me back to reality. He would snicker and keep praying. He nicknamed me Sister Peter, since Peter fell asleep in the garden while Jesus was in intercession. Perry has always had some kind of endless energy that was missing from my metabolism.

From the beginning of our marriage, we burned the roads from town to town, with Perry preaching extended revivals that seemed like a spiritual marathon. We have traveled and ministered in thirty-five states. With each revival, we packed the car with clothes, cassettes, books, and duplication equipment. When one revival ended, it was on to the next location. I soon discovered that Perry was a terrible driver, and he would even try to read a book while driving. He would listen to cassette tapes and not pay attention to red lights and stop signs. Finally I decided that, if I became the designated driver, we stood a better chance of getting us there in one piece. This released him to study. Hundreds of sermons were scribbled on notebook paper during those times.

Usually a small room became our home away from home for weeks on end. Perry studied in the room or at the church most of the day. By the grace of God, I easily adjusted to road travel and to living away from home for weeks at a time. I have many pleasant memories of staying in ministers' homes, where the pastor and his wife made us feel welcome and part of the family. I only recall one occasion when I was uncomfortable staying in a pastor's home.

My favorite state for us to visit was Alabama, since it is my home state where my family and many of my closest friends live. For years, some of our greatest revivals were in Alabama—Sumiton, Adamsville, Northport, Anniston, and many other cities. Still today, some of our closest friends and long-time partners remain those we met during the early revivals in that state.

For a husband and wife to evangelize and minister in local churches, there must be a specific grace of God on their lives and ministry. In every area of the five-fold ministry (apostle, prophet, pastors, teacher and evangelist), people must have the favor and grace of God to help them fulfill their calling. We have missionary friends traveling to third world countries under dangerous circumstances, and they love the challenge and live for the vision of reaching the unreached in those countries. Others make journeys into dangerous nations to carry the message of Christ. Perry has told many missionaries, "I am not *called* to travel where you do, but I am *burdened* to reach the lost and will help you fulfill your assignment."

To this day, I still enjoy packing up and heading to a city for a major conference. It is all part of the calling of God on my life. While our son Jonathan has no interest in traveling, our daughter Amanda is always ready for any road trip and enjoys the times we travel.

CHAPTER 5

OUR CHILDREN

A s a young girl growing up in Alabama, I had all the hopes and dreams that most little girls have. I wanted to finish school, get married, and have children. And every mother hopes it happens in that order. I didn't date much and had not met anybody I believed I wanted to spend the rest of my life with. But when I met Perry, I knew I had found my "prince charming."

After we married, I had everything planned in my mind. I was twenty at the time, and when I turned twenty-five, I wanted to start having babies. That would give us five years to get established in travel and be ready for the big change that I knew would accompany children. I had taken care of an infant until he was two years old, so I knew what it meant to have the responsibility of caring for a baby.

The year 1986 rolled around and I turned twenty-five. But Perry and I both felt that we should not put an infant on the road with the schedule we were keeping. During revivals we stayed in other people's homes, sometimes for weeks at a time, and we had to consider the possibility that some might not be happy with a child in their home for that length of time—especially a baby that could keep them awake crying at night.

Having children was always in the back of my mind, though. When we went to churches for revivals, I would try to find a baby to love on and help with while we were at that church. During long revivals I would often become attached to the little one, and it was never easy to leave them. As we returned to the same churches year after year, I watched the infants grow into children and then teens. Years later they married and began their own families.

Every year for Christmas, Perry used to buy me a doll, thinking that would satisfy my desire to be a mother. One year he found a store that would take your picture and transfer the image onto fabric, and create a stuffed fabric figure that vaguely resembled the person. I opened a present one year and found that Perry had given me one of those odd-looking dolls that had his face imprinted on it. I told him that this doll thing wasn't working for me. I wanted a living, breathing baby.

Around the beginning of 1989 we decided it might be time to add a little Stone to the family. I thought I was pregnant, but over-the-counter tests were negative. We were on our way home for a few days and stopped by the Skelton's in Northport for a quick visit. While we were there, Perry dreamed of a little girl who said her name was Amanda. When we returned home, I went to the doctor and discovered that I was, indeed, expecting a baby. We were certain this baby would be a girl because God had given Perry a dream and had even heard the girl give her name.

I was six months pregnant when we were in a three-week tent revival with T. L. Lowery in the Washington, D.C. area. Do you know what it's like to be six months pregnant and attend church services under a tent in the summer? I was running tapes and selling products, and I had to take my shoes off every night. By the end of the night, my feet were so swollen that I could not get my shoes back on and had to return to the hotel barefoot.

While staying in the Washington D.C. area, Perry had another dream. We had been looking in a baby name book so we could get an idea for a middle name for Amanda. In this dream, Amanda was pushing a baby stroller with a little girl in the stroller. In the dream, Perry asked Amanda who she was strolling and she said, "Rochelle, your little girl."

Perry woke me up and told me the dream. We looked up the name Rochelle and found that it means, "from a little stone." Perry is a junior, so he is a "little stone." We just knew this meant we were going to have twin girls. We chose Michelle as Amanda's middle name because it rhymed with Rochelle. I look back and laugh at our reasoning.

By faith we painted the nursery pink and had a closet full of dresses. But just weeks before I gave birth, a man to whom we were very close told us that we were going to have a son. We were still sure this would be a girl. But sure enough we had a boy. When our son was born, you can hear me on the video asking Perry, "What are we going to name him?"

The doctor asked, "You don't have a name?"

We didn't name him until that afternoon. We chose to name him Jonathan after Perry's grandfather, John. His middle name is Gabriel because he was born on December 23, 1989—two days before Christmas—which also happened to be one of the coldest days in Cleveland's history.

Finally, after eight years of marriage, we had a child. It was a happy, happy day. We quickly changed the color of the room and the clothes were exchanged for boy's clothes. We had a firstborn son and we were as thrilled as we could be.

When Jonathan was born, we were unable to take him home right away because he had jaundice. He was a tiny 5 pounds and 4 ounces, and when we brought him home, the hospital put him in a Christmas stocking. Perry asked, "Are we supposed to hang him on the fireplace and just look at him?"

The enemy seemed to target Jonathan from the beginning, causing us to pray a continual covering over his life to this day. One afternoon while driving on the interstate through Fort Payne, Alabama, we heard what sounded like an explosion inside the van. The right window behind the front passenger seat had suddenly blown into hundreds of pieces, close to where Jonathan was resting in his car seat. At first we thought someone had shot a gun and the bullet had pierced the window, but nobody was standing along the interstate. It is a mystery to this day. But, thankfully, the flying pieces of glass did not cut Jonathan or end up in his eyes.

Perry and I began to rebuke any spirit or spiritual power that might be assigned to attack Jonathan. Our minds went back to an incident that had occurred when Jonathan was about ten months old. It happened in the early morning of October 31st, 1990. For several months, when Jonathan would go sleep, he would wake up at exactly the same time, 12:30 a.m., crying and shaking. I would get up and hold him. Eventually I placed him between Perry and me in the bed. On that morning I was suddenly awakened by him choking. Immediately I turned on the bedside lamp and saw that he had vomited. Then I noticed two distinct marks of blood on the left and right side of his head, as though someone had smeared their bloody fingers across both of his temples. We checked Jonathan, and he was not bleeding anywhere else and had not cut himself or used his own hands to place blood on his temples.

Since this happened on a night that is recognized in the occult, Perry felt that some type of spirit had entered the house and targeted our son. He got out of bed and walked through the house, rebuking the powers of darkness, telling them that they had no legal right to enter our home and commanding them to leave. After about two weeks of prayer, Jonathan stopped waking up at 12:30 a.m. and was finally able to sleep.

A third frightening incident happened in Hagerstown, Maryland. Perry was ministering at the Williamsport Church of God and we were staying in a hotel that had two adjoining rooms. I had gone downstairs to do laundry and Perry had his research material scattered in the second room where he was studying. After some time I returned to the other room and hollered to Perry, "Where's Jonathan?" He replied, "He's in the room somewhere." But he was nowhere to be found. He was about two-and-a-half years old, and apparently he had opened the hotel door and walked out.

He was not in the hall and we were both in a panic. We walked the hall to see if we could hear an infant crying from the rooms on the fourth floor. Our minds were racing, thinking that someone had picked him up or kidnapped him. It was the most hopeless and devastating feeling I had ever experienced.

When we went to the elevator to go to the front desk and tell them, we pushed the button to the elevator door. It opened, and there stood

Jonathan inside the elevator looking at us. He had gotten into the elevator but did not push any buttons. He said he left the room to come looking for me. You can imagine how relieved we were to find that he was safe.

When Jonathan was young, he would always stay behind the resource table with me, because in those days I ran the cassette tapes and sold the materials. It would become very busy behind the table after a service, but Jonathan knew not to wander off or leave with any strangers. We were ministering at the National Church of God in Fort Washington, Maryland, and people had crowded around the table to purchase materials and ask questions. Jonathan was near the edge of the table when a stranger spotted him and said, "I have been waiting to see this fellow." He watched Jonathan for a moment, and then acted as though he was headed to pick up Jonathan, with his eyes darting toward the door.

Unknown to this man, Lewis Mason, a former secret service agent, had noticed this white man in this predominantly black congregation. He knew most of the people in the church personally, and he had never seen this man before. Lewis kept an eye on him and noticed that he was acting a bit nervous when he spotted Jonathan. Before the man could pick up Jonathan, Lewis rushed over and took Jonathan. The man immediately left and was not seen again.

We began to bring Lewis to our two main conferences to organize and oversee a security team. Lewis was trained to recognize a person who didn't fit or was nervous in the crowd. He could detect any abnormal activity. He was also assigned to watch over our children and me in these meetings. Today we have a security team in all of the meetings and Lewis is still occasionally called upon to assist. He has been connected to our ministry since the late 1980s and lives in Cleveland.

Over the years we have pondered these attacks and others, and wondered why the enemy seemed to have a target set on Jonathan. One answer is that every minister, especially one who has an international ministry, builds a global outreach that must be carried on after his (or her) departure. For example, Moses passed the mantle to Joshua, but Joshua failed to pass the mantle after his death. This caused the children of Israel to backslide against God. There must be leaders in churches and ministries who can carry on. Most ministers desire to see their son active in ministry, and often these sons are fought more intensely because of their *potential* to carry on the ministry.

The second point is that, when a mother's first child is a son, there is a special blessing for that son:

> *"And it came to pass, when Pharaoh was stubborn about letting us go, that the Lord killed all the firstborn in the land of Egypt, both the firstborn of man and the firstborn of beast. Therefore I sacrifice to the Lord all males that open the womb, but all the firstborn of my sons I redeem." – Exodus 13:15 (NKJV)*

> *"Then the LORD spoke to Moses, saying: "Now behold, I Myself have taken the Levites from among the children of Israel instead of every firstborn who opens the womb among the children of Israel. Therefore the Levites shall be Mine, because all the firstborn are Mine. On the day that I struck all the firstborn in the land of Egypt, I sanctified to Myself all the firstborn in Israel, both man and beast. They shall be Mine: I am the LORD." – Numbers 3:11-13 (NJKV)*

There are millions of parents whose firstborn child was male. In most families, if parents have two children, one is often compliant and the other defiant; one is obedient and the other is disobedient. For many Christian parents, their firstborn son struggles and seems to be targeted by the enemy from an early age. Under the Law of Moses, the firstborn son was marked for certain blessings that were not given to other children in the family. The firstborn son was promised a double inheritance upon his father's death (Deut. 21:17), and he received an impartation of a special blessing prior to the father's death (Gen. 49).

The youth in this generation, all of whom are living with the promise of a worldwide outpouring of the Holy Spirit, are often targeted by Satan's attacks in his effort to prevent them from fulfilling their destiny. This is especially true with ministers' children. Never stop praying for your children—for those who are living and for those who are still seeds in their father's loins (Heb. 7:10).

Jonathan lived on the road, practically glued to his position in a car seat while we traveled. He endured hours of sitting. Since he needed to be fed and have his diaper changed, we stopped about every two hours for a break. Our little boy grew up traveling away from home and living in hotel rooms. He developed a habit of staying up late with his dad. Sometimes he would go to bed between two and three o'clock a.m. Due to the time Perry spent in study and prayer, playtime with Jonathan and Perry was from eleven o'clock p.m. until two o'clock a.m. He would play games, tell Jonathan stories or jokes, or maybe watch a cartoon video. We lived in a hotel room for as long as the revival lasted.

One of the cutest things Jonathan would do when he was between four and seven years old was run to the platform after the service and grab his dad's Bible and notebook, and carry it back to the office where his dad was changing clothes. Perry would beam with pride to see his little boy holding that big Bible and notebook, guarding it like it was a precious toy. Perry would pick him up and toss him in the air as Jonathan giggled with joy. As he grew, the toss was changed to a hug and a kiss. One of Perry's most unforgettable moments was when little Jonathan looked up at him and said, "Dad, you're my hero!"

Jonathan traveled with us from the age of one month to the age of eleven years and was homeschooled, until he finally asked if he could attend a private school in the area. We allowed him to do that, which meant that I had to stop traveling so much with Perry. He had to put together staff to travel to the meetings with him, which he still does today.

Ten years after Jonathan was born, I was thirty-eight years old and Perry and I decided that it was time for us to start thinking about those two little girls Perry had seen in his dream eleven years earlier. It wouldn't be too many more years before I wouldn't be able to have more children. Time was slipping by, and if we were going to have more children, we needed to do it soon.

By this time we had the Manna-fest program, and Perry was not holding four to eleven week revivals. So I got pregnant, expecting the daughter that Perry had dreamed about.

I was about eight weeks into the pregnancy and the doctor saw the first sign of complications—no heartbeat. Right away they wanted me to terminate the pregnancy. I refused, so they agreed to give me a few more weeks, thinking that maybe I wasn't as far along as they thought.

I prayed and asked God to let the baby live. One morning while praying, I heard the Lord ask me, "Do you want me to let this baby live, no matter what condition it is in?"

That was a shocking question. So I decided to start praying for God's will to be done. A few weeks later, we were at the Main Event Conference in Pigeon Forge when I had a miscarriage.

God is faithful, though, and two months later on Christmas Eve, I learned that I was pregnant again. Perry began to tell me, "It is a girl and she's Amanda. Watch and see if this is not the girl I saw in those dreams." This time the dream would become a reality, and on August 2, 2001 Amanda Michelle was born. Having a little girl was everything I thought it would be, including frilly dresses, baby dolls, and playing dress up. She has brought much joy to us in our later years. She has kept us young, that's for sure. Amanda loves the Lord and she is involved in the OCI drama and dance team, Audience of One.

Each day Perry and I speak over our children in prayer and make confessions on their behalf. Perry has tried to emphasize to them the importance of keeping a heart of repentance toward God and of always picking themselves up if they fail in any manner. We pray that both will follow Christ and enter the kingdom where they will hear Christ say, "Well done, good and faithful servant."

We love our children very much. They have very different personalities from each other, but God has a work for each of them that nobody else can do. We pray over them each day that they will fulfill the call that God has on their lives.

What about the other little girl Rochelle, you ask? Perry and I have discussed this many times, and we don't know how to answer that question. Maybe she was the baby we lost to miscarriage.

This is an area where we simply must trust God and believe that He knows all things and is in control of our lives and the lives of our children. We believe that the soul and spirit of a child enters the womb at the moment of conception, and we know that we have a child in heaven who will be waiting on us. Perhaps the infant that didn't have a chance to be born on earth was our little Rochelle.

Perry said that in the dream, Rochelle did not look as healthy as Amanda. She seemed weak in her physical appearance. He sensed in the dream that Rochelle might be deaf and unable to speak, as Amanda was speaking for her. I can only surmise about this. Rather than question, we thank God for the two wonderful children He gave us. They have also made a sacrifice to have a dad who travels most week-ends and often misses being with the family on Mother's Day, Father's Day, Thanksgiving (because of Israel tours) and other special occasions. It all comes with the territory, though, when Dad is an evangelist who travels. It's part of living in two worlds.

CHAPTER 6

A MAN WHO LIVES IN TWO WORLDS

OST MINISTERS LIVE in two different worlds. As an evangelist, my husband lives in one world that is spiritual. In this world he is expected to minister to people under an anointing, bring forth a message through the Word and Spirit of God, and pray for people at the altars. He won't succeed at this unless he spends much time in study and prayer before he stands behind the pulpit. In the case of a pastor, he must be a shepherd to the flock seven days a week, twenty-four hours a day if necessary. When that minister comes home, he is now a husband and a dad, living in the natural world. But he has been in two worlds that day.

He has spoken to a church full of people and brought a word from the Lord that was birthed through much study and prayer. He had to press into the Kingdom of God to hear the voice of the heavenly Father reveal a message from the throne room—a message the Lord wanted released to the congregation.

All men of God are still just men. He must move from one world to the next quickly, once he returns home as a man with a wife and children. As God's minister, he will hear and speak the eternal Word of the Lord; but as a husband, he will come home and his family now wants his ear. As a minister, he will dedicate infants and impart prayers of destiny; but as Dad, he returns home and tucks his own children in bed and prays over them before they go to sleep. As a man of God, he might carry a strong anointing that will cause demonic powers to flee; but as a husband, he will submit to a rebuke from his wife who loves him and is protecting him from possible threat and danger.

As God's representative, he will pray for the sick and see them recover. But as a human being, he is subject to sickness and will one day die, and no prayer will prevent his departure when it is time for him to go. He is anointed; but just as David said about himself, at times he is weak, although he is anointed for ministry (2 Sam. 3:29).

His wife and children know him better than anyone else. I say this about any minister's wife and not just myself. It takes a call of God and a special grace to live with a man of two worlds.

Men and women called of God can never stop having an ear to hear, even when they are not behind the pulpit. There is hearing with the *natural* ear and hearing with the *spiritual* ear. When it comes to hearing with the natural ear, here is something that annoys me. I think I am like most wives when I say that, when I am talking to my husband, I want his attention. I don't want to talk to somebody who is focused on typing on the computer while I'm trying to tell them something. I want him to stop, make eye contact, and listen. This is an area that still requires work, and I make him stop what he is doing and make eye contact when I am speaking.

Hearing with the spiritual ear is something he does well, though. I saw this in action the first time Perry returned to Northport Church of God for a second revival, a year following his first one. After service the young people were eating at Taco Casa. Perry was at the counter ordering when he invited a young man, Kenny Trawick, to attend the revival one night. I had gone to high school with Kenny.

After the invitation, Kenny looked at Perry and said, "I would come but I'm working tomorrow night." Perry didn't blink an eye when he shot back, "If you lie, you fry!" He took his food and sat down, leaving Kenny with a blank stare on his face. Kenny had lied to Perry, but he became so convicted that he showed up at the revival and accepted Christ. He remained faithful, and today he pastors a dynamic, growing church in Connecticut.

Perry has walked in a store to order food, and while standing in line the Lord might say, "The girl serving you needs fifty dollars." He would pay for the food and say, "The Lord told me you needed fifty dollars." The girl would cry and confess that she had prayed that God would give her money for gas because her tank was empty and she had no money. On a few occasions, we have given away vehicles, furniture, and other items to assist someone in need, as our blessings come from obedience, and giving as the Lord instructs has always been a part of our lives.

Those who knew Perry's dad, Fred, often said they had never met a minister who had a more sensitive ear to the voice of the Holy Spirit than he did. Fred lived a life of prayer that opened his ears toward the inner voice of the Holy Spirit, imparting to him spiritual knowledge and revelation. Time and time again he would say, "Many people know how to talk to God, but not many know how to hear from God." I believe Perry also has ears to hear as he listens to the Lord's direction.

Marrying a minister of the Gospel means that the wife lives with a man who lives in two worlds. But as I have said many times, I am humbled and honored that God would select me to be Perry's wife.

BALANCING AN UNBALANCED PREACHER

At times people will ask me, "Of all the places you have been, what's your favorite city and your favorite church?" This is a difficult question to answer, as I have enjoyed most places we have traveled. We have met many wonderful people, including pastors, and their wives, and we have experienced the joy of watching the Holy Spirit move in the revivals and conferences. However, when looking back, I believe the city and church that I have enjoyed most during our years of ministry and travel would be the city of Baltimore and the Edgemere Church of God.

Perry and I were invited to Edgemere in the mid-1980s. The church is located just outside of Baltimore, Maryland and when we were there, the church was pastored by Rev. Howard Hancock. During our visits we stayed in the home of Pastor Hancock and his wife Naomi, also enjoying the company of their two children, Suzi and Todd.

This was my favorite place for several reasons. First, the church members at Edgemere were a wonderful group of people, and we saw great spiritual results in the services, year after year. The Hancock's were so much fun to stay with, and Naomi made plans to do something every day, usually around lunchtime. Maryland is also known for its seafood, and Perry and I (as well as our children) enjoy fresh seafood. Another reason I looked forward to being with the Hancocks was because Pastor Howard was the *only* pastor who could break Perry's routine and get him out of the house to enjoy the scenery or some interesting places in the area.

Naomi made plans the night before and she might say, "Tomorrow at eleven o'clock we will leave and go to the harbor." The next night she might strategize, "Tomorrow we need to leave about ten-thirty to get to Pennsylvania to eat at the farmhouse and still have plenty of time to get back."

As we discussed the plans, Perry would interject, "I'm not going anywhere. I have to study and pray for the service." Pastor Hancock would have both hands in his pants pockets and say, "You're too unbalanced. You need some balance in your life. You spend too much time locked up in a room and you need to get out with Pam and have a life."

Perry would try to argue his point, but he always lost because he was outnumbered three to one. I would say, "Come on and get out. God's not going to kill you if you enjoy life a little bit."

So Perry would give in, and then study after the evening service until around two o'clock in the morning. The next day we would be gone for about two or three hours and still make it back in plenty of time to prepare for the service.

I think Pastor Hancock was so adamant about Perry relaxing and experiencing a change now and then because of something that occurred at the church during an extended revival. Perry had been preaching for several weeks and had been complaining to me that he felt unusually tired, to the point of exhaustion. It was Sunday night, going into the second week of the revival. That night he was about fifteen minutes into the message when he stopped abruptly and closed his Bible. Placing most of his weight upon the pulpit, he leaned over and said, "Folks, I cannot finish this message. My strength has completely gone out of me." He slid to the floor.

It was so abrupt, the congregation didn't know if he was having a heart attack or a physical collapse. I was very concerned, as I had never seen him this way before. The pastor took the microphone and asked the church to begin to pray for Perry and to have a time of intercession. A roar filled the church as people began to pray.

Then something very touching happened with a young girl, about nine years of age, who loved Perry's preaching and always came with her parents, never missing a service. Without asking permission, she made her way to the pulpit, where by now Perry was on his face groaning. The young girl placed her hand on Perry's back and began to cry and shake as she prayed in the Holy Spirit. She was just a child with a sincere prayer, but she stayed there about thirty minutes and prayed for him.

Perry later said that he felt a hand on his back, but had no idea who it was. He said he knew someone was praying, and at first it was just a faith prayer and he didn't feel different physically. However, he said that as the prayer continued, he began to sense a Divine energy that filled his body and slowly washed away the intense weariness and exhaustion. He experienced a supernatural renewal that brought him back to his feet and the revival continued for another week without hindrance.

In the service that night was a man who knew a lot about physical fitness and training. He knew that Perry was following a heavy itinerary, and he also noticed that he perspired heavily when he preached. In those days Perry wore a black suit with a black vest, and many times after the service the back of the vest was soaking wet with a white, chalk-like substance. It was salt. The man observed this and asked him, "Do you take vitamins, and do you eat a lot of vegetables and fruits?" Of course the answer was no.

He instructed Perry to change his eating habits. He also said, "You need to replenish the electrolytes in your body, as they are depleted night after night." He suggested that Perry take a bottle of Gatorade to the pulpit. From that time on and for years to come, Perry drank a sports drink after the service to replenish his electrolytes.

It would be easy to blame his physical weakness on the devil. But even Jesus needed time to rest and refresh himself. Perry's lack of strength was due to him pushing beyond his limitations and not understanding the body's needs for mineral replenishment. The same is true concerning another area where he physically struggled in the earlier part of his ministry—his voice.

In February of 1980, during the Northport revival, we all noticed that Perry would bring a glass of something to the pulpit. While he preached, he would reach under the pulpit and take a few swigs. After several services and much curiosity, he held up the glass and told us, "So you'll know, this is not moonshine. It's water, lemon juice and honey for my throat."

For several years, he would start to lose his voice by the end of the service, especially during the winter months. Again, it would be easy to pin the blame on the adversary, who was trying to take the preacher's voice to shut his mouth.

One night toward the conclusion of the revival, an older minister observed Perry struggling with his voice. Noticing how he perspired while preaching, he approached Perry and asked, "When you are finished preaching, do you change your shirt and blow your hair dry?" Perry replied that he did neither. The minister said, "Here is why you are having vocal trouble. You are going out into the cold air after preaching, with a wet shirt and the pores of your head open from where you have been sweating. If you will change your shirt and blow your hair dry, it will stop your vocal problems." From then on, Perry carried a change of shirt and a blow dryer to spare his voice.

If you attend a service or a conference where Perry is ministering, you will notice that shortly after the altar service begins, he will leave. Some have thought Perry was exiting the sanctuary to keep from meeting people or mingling with attendees. This is not the reason. If he remains in the sanctuary with the air conditioner blowing, or if he cools off with air blowing on his head, he will have difficulty with his voice in the following service. Since 1980, he has done this to ensure that he does not lose his voice before the next service.

He has also commented that it takes about twenty minutes for the anointing to subside, and he will remain in the office for a period of time to flow from the anointing back to the normal realm. He says, "I can't explain this, but if I am moving from the anointing during the service to a normal mode after the service, I can't be interrupted with conversation or distractions during that time. If I am, I cannot think clearly and I become frustrated." Once he returns to normal, he is ready to enjoy the fellowship of those around him.

Ministers are men of God, but they are also men who live in physical bodies with limitations. Their body needs to be refreshed and replenished. Certainly the adversary would love to stick a "thorn in the flesh" in every minister to hinder his voice and ministry. However, at times the hindrance may be something we *aren't* doing that we should be doing, or something we *are* doing that we shouldn't be doing.

We have heard of ministers who suffer from heart disease or some other form of physical affliction that was brought upon them, not by the devil, but by poor eating habits, stress, or a lack of exercise. At times these afflictions have led to an early retirement or a premature death.

One thing we learn as we get older is that we must take better care of ourselves as we age. If you look in the mirror and hate your excess weight, there is something you can do about it. You can exercise and change your diet. When traveling, you adjust to another person's schedule and eating habits. This can be a challenge, because it is not easy to change old habits. But we can pray for the Lord to help us discipline our eating habits or other things we need to do in an effort to improve our lives.

When any minister pushes his physical body, his mental strength, or his emotions to the limit, it is possible to hit a wall of physical exhaustion, emotional burnout, or spiritual deadness. During Perry's ministry there have been three times when we were concerned about a condition known as adrenal fatigue. This is a condition in which the adrenal glands cannot meet the demands of stress a person is living under. I have told him for years that he often pushes a schedule beyond normal limits; then after many months, he will suddenly find himself without the strength to function physically. One time he didn't have the strength to get out of bed for two days. Another time, he was walking outside for exercise when his strength left him and he called Robbie James to pick him up and drive him back to the office.

During these times, the only relief is to be refilled and replenished in body, soul and spirit. After these incidents, Perry has learned to take time and rest, and realize the letter "S" in his last name stands for Stone and not Superman. Ministers must learn to do as Jesus did, and come apart for a while before they come apart.

There must be a balance between these two worlds—maintaining a walk in the Spirit and ears to hear, and then living as a husband, father, and friend in a natural world that demands a human response to human needs. When the Apostle Paul traveled throughout Asia, he met other believers who refreshed him. This refreshing or inner rest will help bridge the spiritual and natural worlds.

CHAPTER 7

SWEATING PEANUTS
IN A CONTROVERSY

B EFORE I WRITE this chapter, I want to preface my comments. Both Perry and I have a background in the same denomination, and we have great respect for the many godly, wonderful people who are part of this group. We would never trade our church experiences and the memories we made for anything, and we always pray that the organization will follow the plan of God until the return of Christ.

Our ministry today, however, is inter-denominational. We minister in various churches and denominations, bridging denominational gaps and uniting ministers in fellowship. This information I'm going to share is part of our life story and deals with what we feel was, at times, unnecessary criticism, and at other times, verbal persecution that we had to endure for many years.

In the earlier years of the ministry, when Perry was in his 20s and 30s, he preached successful revivals at nearly every location. However, if you were to ask someone within our denomination, "What do you think of Perry Stone?" there were no middle-of-the-road answers. Either you enjoyed his ministry or you thought he was too controversial. I never understood why some thought he was controversial, because his messages were biblically sound, the anointing was always present, and there were wonderful results in the altars. But over time, I discovered their reasons for thinking he was controversial.

We both came from a strict Pentecostal denomination that established certain requirements for their members to follow. These were practical commitments meant to guard members against entrapment of the enemy and to strengthen them against carnal, worldly pleasures. Most of the people who joined a local church had a strong desire to live as close to God and as far from the world's sinful influence as possible, so they adhered to these practical commitments.

When Perry first began his ministry, there was an unwritten rule that, if you were licensed or ordained within our denomination, you did not conduct revivals in other denominations. Perry's thinking was that, if Jesus said go into the entire world and preach the Gospel to every creature, this would include every denomination. When he began to receive invitations to minister in other denominations, this did not set well with some pastors and denominational leaders. Some feared that a revival would break out in the other church and cause some of their members to attend that church.

Throughout the years, we would minister at an independent or a Charismatic congregation and word would come to us that a pastor in the area (within our own denomination) had stood before his congregation on a Sunday morning and told his members not to attend Perry's revival, giving some odd reason for their instruction. Thus the first controversy was brewed by ministers who believed that an evangelist should minister only in his own denomination.

The second controversy seems trivial today, but after visiting Israel and learning the incredible link between Hebraic roots and Christianity, along with new prophetic information coming from the nation, we were astonished at how little Christians really knew about the Bible and their own religion. For instance, Christians knew nothing about the Feasts of the Lord and their connection to Christ's redemptive ministry, or how the feasts conceal future events. We didn't even understand the different forms of rejoicing and worship linked to the foundation of the Old Testament.

Once Perry gains illumination that he was unfamiliar with, he is like a race horse coming out of the gate at a derby. This happened after he went to Israel. He returned to America and began teaching Hebraic roots. At that time, there were very few people preaching this subject. Most ministers would preach primarily from the New Testament, because they viewed the Old Testament as part of the Old Covenant and thought it was all done away with through Christ.

Not only was Perry building messages around the prophecies, patterns, types, and shadows from the Old Testament; he was also explaining the significance of shofars, banners, dancing before the Lord, and rejoicing as a reaction to worship. He taught the difference between dancing in the Spirit and dancing before the Lord, which caused quite a controversy among traditional ministers. Most of the congregation enjoyed learning these Hebraic insights, but ministers who were unfamiliar with the teachings would tell their people, "I don't believe in that stuff," instead of trying to learn fresh truth.

In 1981, Perry conducted a revival in Daisy, Tennessee that continued for almost eight weeks. Over five hundred were saved in that revival. While there, he was impressed to have people bring an object of any kind to church, and he and others would lay hands upon it and ask God that, when the sinner came in contact with it, conviction of the Holy Spirit would strike their heart. We prayed, and each night, prayers were answered as those sinners came to church and repented at the altar. Time and again, someone would testify that the loved one who accepted Christ had been in contact with whatever we had agreed over in prayer.

In the fourth week of the revival, the pastor received a phone call from someone in a high leadership position, demanding that Perry stop doing this because he felt there was "no Bible for it." Perry reminded him that Jesus said, "If two of you shall agree as touching any*thing*, it would be done," and that Perry was praying over *things*. But this person in authority was not thrilled that people were being saved; he was more concerned about the method than the results.

This caused even more controversy. Word spread and people said, "He is praying over all kinds of things and that's heresy." But critics were seldom informed of testimonies of conviction and salvation, nor did they consider the fact that Paul's handkerchiefs were used as a point of contact to bring healing to the sick (Acts 19:12). When reminding people of this Scripture, Perry was told that he was not Paul, and Paul's method was just for the early church.

During this time, we were members of a large and respected church in Cleveland, where Perry had ministered on several occasions. A shift occurred in the mid-1980s, after he preached a four-week revival in Lenoir City, Tennessee. We felt at that time that we should transfer our membership from the Cleveland church to the Highland Hills church, which was about forty-five minutes away from our home. This church was already strong in Hebraic teaching, and they owned a television studio where Perry taped his videos. The church also had numerous outreaches that we desired to support with our tithes and offerings.

This happened during the latter part of the Charismatic movement, and there were doctrinal clashes between the classical Pentecostal and the newer Charismatic denominations. To the critic, the church we joined was too Charismatic. This renewed another series of verbal attacks again us by several leaders who rejected this style of teaching and worship.

We could have become greatly offended and begun a campaign of defending ourselves. But we believe Psalm 37:23—that the footsteps of the righteous are always ordered of the Lord. In the mid-and late-1980s, as ministry doors began shutting in some churches, doors in other churches opened. Everything worked out as God had planned. But I want to illustrate how someone's opinion and words can impact another, and harm their reputation based on false opinions.

Perry received an exhorter's certificate at age seventeen and was accepted as a licensed minister in Virginia at age eighteen. This made him one of the youngest licensed ministers in the state of Virginia in the denomination's history. Because of the many extended revivals that brought spiritual results, at age twenty-one, he was invited to preach at the North Cleveland Church of God, which was the most noted Church of God in America.

That revival brought attention to his ministry. It led to invitations from state overseers for him to speak at their state camp meetings, a yearly event in which all of the pastors and any members who wanted to attend meet in one location for services. In his early and mid-twenties he preached the Northern Ohio, Maryland and Kentucky State Church of God Camp meetings.

Once we joined the church in Highland Hills, some church leaders who did not believe in Hebraic teaching began to reject any minister or church that used colorful banners, or blew shofars, or expressed worship through dance and drama teams. They criticized anything that appeared to be Jewish or Old Testament. They set out to ensure that Perry would never preach in the larger meetings again. They were saying, "He has gone off the deep end. We had such hopes for him, but he has blown it."

In a closely knit denomination, word spreads quickly. On the flip side, there were many ministers who continued to invite Perry to their church every year and just ignored the opinions of others. But there was still plenty of ammunition being shot at him. Because of this, he was known as the "controversial minister."

Perry began to question whether he should stay with this denomination. He would say, "It's crazy to stay connected to a denomination with so many leaders and ministers who treat me like an outcast because I preach things they're not familiar with. It is like working for a company that wants to fire you, but they won't because they benefit from your work."

During this time, we were ministering at the Pentecostal Holiness camp ground in Dublin, Virginia when a Bishop from the Assembly of God denomination from a neighboring state asked to meet with Perry privately. This state leader sat with Perry and began questioning him about his ministry and connection with our denomination. The minister said, "Perry, would you consider joining the Assemblies of God?" This bishop noted that there was a void in their denomination (with the moral failure of their leading evangelist), and he believed that, if Perry would unite with their fellowship, many doors would open for national and international ministry. As well, the Assembly of God had nearly identical beliefs as the Church of God.

We discussed this and considered the possibility. Perry had four generations of ministers in the family, and his grandfather, John Bava, and his father, Fred Stone, were both ordained in the Church of God denomination. Perry knew that if he left the denomination, his grandfather would be grieved. Perry's family had deep roots and friendships in the denomination. He does not forsake his friends, even in the toughest times. I reminded him, "The grass is not always greener on the other side. Anywhere that you have people and ministers, you will make friends and create opposition. Let's just stay where we are."

He prayed about it and felt that he should stay. He said, "If I ever make a transition in the future, it will be when things are going great, and when I can make the transition in peace and not confusion." He decided to hang around and preach, and keep tormenting the people who didn't like all that Hebraic Old Testament teaching.

In the latter 1980s, when we began to host our yearly Main Event conference in Pigeon Forge, Perry invited the Hebriac Worship and Arts team from our church in Highland Hills to present worship from a Hebraic perspective. This represented the original form of worship in biblical times, the same worship you see in Israel today, and the style of worship that will exist the millennial reign of Christ. We did this long before these subjects were popular to teach. At that time, they were not widely accepted in the body of Christ, but they are today.

You should have seen the expressions on some of the precious, more traditional church folks when woman came out dressed in white flowing robes and began a pageantry of celebration with tambourines and banners. The style of worship was different, but the atmosphere was anointed. However, some were unwilling to move beyond their present understanding and expand their thinking to include something that they considered a "new thing." It is always easier for some to stay comfortable in tradition than to be challenged. For us, it was hard to imagine how you can prove something from the Bible, but people still refuse to accept it because it confronts their comfort zone or challenges their traditions.

Now look ahead to today. About half the Manna-fest programs are taped in Israel. Many of Perry's books and teachings deal with insight into Hebraic teaching. Millions of people are grateful that he endured the opposition, remained faithful to the call, and has continued to be a voice in this area of study. Throughout the world, the Manna-fest programs and Perry's teachings have allowed Christians to understand the Hebraic roots of Christianity, and these believers are enjoying the fruit of those studies.

Back in the days when Perry's ministry was enduring verbal assault, he had three spiritual mentors: his father, Rev. Floyd Lawhon, and Dr. T. L. Lowery, who was elected an assistant General Overseer in Cleveland within our denomination. Dr. Lowery admired Perry, and he often said, "When I see Perry in that black suit with that black hair, pacing the platform and preaching, it reminds me of myself in my early days." Other people would say that Perry is another T. L. Lowery, which we both considered a high compliment.

Perry traveled to a meeting where Dr. Lowery was ministering, and after service he invited Perry to the hospitality room. They talked about thirty minutes. Well, actually Perry talked about thirty minutes. He told of the verbal assaults, and how he felt they were a character assassination. He complained about how ministers could treat other ministers in such a terrible manner and still say they love God.

At the conclusion of Perry's rant, he was expecting to hear profound words. And he did. Dr. Lowery leaned over the table and said: "Don't sweat the peanuts."

Perry said nothing. He thought, "What in the world is that supposed to mean?"

Dr. Lowery explained, "Don't sweat because of what people say. Keep yourself out there before the people, even if you are controversial. Throughout my entire ministry people have called me controversial. Don't waste your energy defending yourself. Stay humble before God and the day will come in the future when the very people who don't like you will come out to hear you preach."

These words turned out to be true. As the years have progressed and our ministry has gone from the local, rural churches in America to over 250 nations of the world, some of Perry's closest friends and supporters are the Bishops within the denomination. Many have listened to his messages and gleaned insight. Today in most churches, there is an understanding of Hebraic roots, and some pastors are now teaching this. All has come full circle. And thankfully, Perry chose not to sweat the peanuts. These lessons should teach us all to obey, remain calm in adversity, and allow God to fight our battles for us.

It has always been important for me as a wife to also be both his critic and encourager. Most wives know that many men tend to pout or become discouraged under certain circumstances. This is when the woman must step up and encourage him. At the same time, she must be able to lovingly correct him when needed.

WHY DID YOU SAY THAT?

While Perry never sought to be controversial, there were a few times when he would be preaching and say something that would make me think, "Oh no! Why did you say that?" I have been listening to my husband preach for decades, including the two-and-a-half years before he was my husband. He doesn't preach a boring or an uninteresting message. He spends at least six to eight hours a day in the office, digging into the Word and researching whatever topic the Holy Spirit places on his heart to preach. But sometimes a sermon might go on and on, like the Boston Marathon, or sometimes he uses a phrase or makes a statement that makes me cringe.

One example was a message he preached at the Main Event in Pigeon Forge, which is a yearly conference that we started hosting at the OCI facility in Cleveland in 2013. This was our most anticipated and largest attended conference of the year.

Perry was just learning how the fall feasts conceal prophetic events. He was so excited about the message, which was titled something like, "Rosh Hashanah, the Day of Atonement, and the Resurrection." Just the title alone was a red flag that he was getting ready to preach too many messages in one, and he was going to attempt this in one hour. There is a word for that: impossible.

The praise and worship and all preliminaries were over in about thirty-five minutes. And then came the message...and the message... and the message...that we determined was the eternal, never-ending sermon. He preached for two hours and thirty minutes, seemingly without taking a breath. People looked like deer staring into head-lights. They were not drawn by the content; they were comatose from confusion. At that time, only a few people understood the feasts, and Perry wasn't helping matters.

When we returned to the hotel room, I was preparing food for the ministry team when I turned to Perry and said, "You could have left out the first hour of the message. Nobody understood it." He looked at me and said, "Maybe you didn't, but I'm sure the other people did."

I wanted to prove my gut feeling. So when the team—about twenty people—arrived in our suite, I asked them for an honest opinion. "Did you understand the first hour of the message?"

They looked like they had been caught and were going to be in big trouble if they answered. They looked at Perry, then at me, then at Perry and said, "Well...maybe...well, some...well...." One person who was always completely honest said, "It was totally confusing!" We all laughed.

But Perry was concerned that he had not properly communicated the message, so from that moment, he began to reorganize his Hebraic and prophetic information. He would discuss the content with some of the people at the office, knowing that if he could explain it in simple enough terms that they would understand, then the people in the con-ference would understand it, too. He would ask Gina Bean to listen to his explanation on certain subjects. If she looked puzzled, he would ask, "What didn't you get?" He would explain the content again until she replied; "Now I get it."

The following year at this same conference, many of the people in attendance had also been there the year before. Perry remembered what I said about that sermon the previous year, and he wanted to demonstrate to me that only a few of us did not fully comprehend the first hour. On opening night he asked how many people were present the previous year on Saturday night. Many hands shot up. He said,

"Now be honest. How many of you did not understand the first part of the message I preached?" After a brief pause, hands came up slowly, some at half-mast as if to avoid being seen by others. I smiled, knowing I was right about that one.

This was a useful lesson for him to learn, because when he presents little-known information, the listener wants to understand it.

Then sometimes, he says things he could have left out. For our first ten years of ministry, Perry preached primarily in traditional Pentecostal churches. These were wonderful people, but we soon learned that these folks were often very traditional in their style of worship, their music, and the type of preaching they wanted to hear. If anyone—and I believe anyone would include Jesus Himself—came to their church and did one thing to wreck the routine, they would have been certain God was preparing lightning bolts to strike the offender dead before midnight.

In those earlier days, if women who were not affiliated with this church came to the revival dressed in pants, or wearing makeup or jewelry, church members griped because they believed these "Jezebels" were corrupting the congregation. Songs had to be sung only from the red-backed hymnal or the people were ready to pick up rocks and stone someone. Church members would even get upset if a visitor sat in the seat they had occupied for years. On one occasion I watched a row of visitors being asked to get up and sit somewhere else, as they were sitting in the seat of a charter member. They did get up. And they walked right out the door.

Perry and I were fine with certain traditions, but when a tradition hindered the flow of the Holy Spirit or stopped people from loving a visitor or a sinner, neither one of us had patience for it. He would make a sincere attempt to help the people see this during the revival, by using the Word of God to point out how that certain traditions could be a hindrance. He wanted them to see that the church could be more effective and have greater impact in the community if the members would love these newcomers and sinners instead of judging them.

When Perry sensed that the people didn't appreciate being told this, their stubborn response would fire him up even more. He would defend his stance, causing some people to get up and walk out. Others would fold their arms and stare him down. After years of this, he would tell people, "I got victory a long time ago over the way some of you stare at me, so smile. It might shock your neighbor." Perry would get fired up trying to get people to see the light, and the people in the pews would become equally fired up. Soon "fiery darts" were flying from the pulpit to the pew and the pew to the pulpit. If looks could kill, he would have dropped dead many times.

The Holy Spirit finally spoke to Perry and said, "Quit trying to change these people. I could not change the children of Israel after forty years in the wilderness, and you won't do it in three weeks. Just preach the Word and minister to those who are hungry."

That is when Perry stopped trying to change the traditions of people who had been living with them a lifetime. He focused on content and the anointing of the Holy Spirit. Sometimes the very people who were most resistant began to break when the fire of God started to fall in the congregation. Over time, he had to learn that what you don't say is as important as what you do say, and the tone in which you say it is as important as your content.

He was influenced by watching the actions of Pastor Joe Edwards, who helped Perry from the time he was a single preacher. Joe could rebuke a person with such love that people would be thanking him when it was over. We often said that Joe is the only man who could call someone into his office and fire them, and have them feeling great when they walked out the door. Joe always taught to weigh your words carefully before you speak them, use wisdom in knowing when to speak, and watch the tone in which you speak. Joe used to say, "When Perry was younger, people were astonished at his preaching. But you really never knew what he might say at any minute."

I suppose this was another reason he was considered controversial. His approach to certain traditions was more vigorous than you heard from most ministers. People who knew Perry back then would all agree that he has toned it down quite a bit from his younger years. Age and experience has brought maturity.

Perry was also controversial because of the content of some messages. Over the years, the Lord has directed him to preach messages with unusual or difficult themes—particularly prophetic messages. Three such messages were The Apparitions of Mary–the Missing Link; The American-Egyptian Prophetic Parallels; and Unleashing the Beast. These messages taught insight about how specific current events parallel certain prophecies, and how those events could fulfill those prophecies.

Each time he preached one of these messages, we encountered strange and unusual warfare. Unleashing the Beast was a revelation from the Holy Spirit for this generation, because it identified the future antichrist as being from an Islamic background. When Perry preached this on television, strange things occurred. On the Daystar Network in Dallas, the power in the television station—just the station and nowhere else—went out for no reason in the middle of an important point. In the same studio, as he was preparing notes before the live telecast, a heavy light fixture came crashing down on the table near his head—again, for no apparent reason. He could have been maimed or killed had it struck him on the head. At other places, unexpected lightning would blow up sound boards, storms would knock out electricity, and other forms of odd warfare would break out.

Years ago, during our first Spiritual Warfare Conference hosted in Tampa, Florida, about two hours before church service, storm clouds rolled over the city. We stood at the balcony window of the high rise hotel and could see the church, which was about a mile away. We counted forty sky-to-ground lightning strikes, all on or around the church property. The Daystar satellite truck was parked on the property, and an alarm when off, causing the engineer to run from the truck to the inside of the church. A power surge blew out half of the sound system, and this happened one hour before the opening service.

Each night, one hour before the service began, the sky above the city would become a raging lightning show, often striking and blowing up transformers and affecting power in the area. The news reported that this was the most severe weather and lightning on record in Tampa.

For many years, Perry chose not to publicly announce the titles of his messages, especially if they dealt with strong warfare, exposing Satan's kingdom, or any prophetic theme related to Islam. He had observed that, if he announced certain messages the night before, the next day all kinds of things would happen to keep people from attending. We noticed a distinct change in these attacks only when our head intercessor, Bea Ogle, began having hundreds of women, through the Daughters of Rachel prayer ministry, begin to pray against satanic-inspired assaults. We believe their prayers built hedges against demonic opposition and provided angelic protection.

Without a doubt, the most difficult and controversial messages are those that deal with America's prophetic patterns. When a message exposes the parallels of America with ancient empires, it is common to connect the leaders in America with patterns of the leaders in those ancient biblical empires. In November of 1992, Perry taught that the Ahab and Jezebel spirit was coming to America. This proved to be true under the Clinton administration. He spoke of the patterns of President Bush and the unusual parallels after the election was thrown into confusion. With President Obama, he taught the patterns with the Egyptian Pharaoh who "knew not Joseph."

People anticipate Perry's sermons about America and the nation's prophetic patterns; but before the message concludes, it is typical for between four and a dozen people to walk out offended. Sometimes he jokes, "We had a good service tonight. I didn't lose anyone."

These messages are important to the nation and to the church, but they are difficult to preach because they can be misunderstood and offensive to some—especially to people who support a particular administration or point of view. Perry only wants to present the truth and help people, but as he reveals a biblical truth and prophetic parallel, some get offended. He calls them selective believers, because they find comfort in picking and choosing what they want to believe, and throwing away whatever challenges their traditions or way of thinking.

A few times I've been concerned about information he shared. At a summer conference in Saint Louis, he was speaking about individuals, as far back as 1973, who had attempted to hinder nationally-known ministries, even setting them up in an attempt to destroy their integrity. He exposed two incidents that had not been publicized that revealed how certain groups in Washington were targeting those who had influence in the nation. The government feared that these ministers could influence voting, especially on certain social issues, and thus the liberals wanted to silence their voices.

The message must have stirred up something big. The next morning, security personnel observed two federal vehicles in the parking lot. When the people in the cars were approached, they said they were interested in speaking to Perry. Later, they left without any discussion.

When we returned home, the ministry website had been hacked, and the damage was so severe that nobody in our area could fix it. Men who worked with our host server flew the hard drive to Virginia, where several individuals who were highly skilled in technology recovered information, fixed the problem, and set more firewalls in the system. One person overseeing the project said, "Someone wanted to send him a message." While we cannot definitively link the hack job to someone in our government, under the circumstances, we would not be surprised to find a connection.

We have also learned through several sources that, for many years, some in high levels of authority have been concerned that a minister or ministry could become too influential. The fear is that their influence could motivate a multitude to vote based on spiritual or social issues that could impact the nation. This was exposed in the 1970s when five large ministries were targeted by a few insiders within the U.S. Justice Department. These five were the top ministers in America with a listening audience of tens of millions of Christians.

In the Gospels, Christ's ministry and influence was considered by the Pharisees a threat to their own power and control over the multitudes. The Pharisees were concerned that Christ might cause a rebellion that would lead to the Roman soldiers seizing total control and removing their influence over the Temple and Jerusalem, as mentioned in John 11:46-48. Even though Jesus performed many miracles, they were afraid that if they left Him alone, everybody would believe on Him and the Romans would come and take away their positions.

It is the assignment of the adversary to use people and circumstances to prevent ministers from influencing others for the Kingdom's sake. A minister's wife must remember this and be prepared to stand with her man in the times when these attacks come and the arrows are flying. Like many other ministers in the public eye, we have had to deal with this for years. And we have the battle scars to prove it.

CLEAN BUT MEAN

The phrase, *clean but mean*, describes the outward appearance but inward attitude of the Pharisee sect from Christ's time. They dressed properly and followed the strict interpretation of the Law of Moses and the traditions of the elders, but they had no compassion toward sinners and no mercy toward anyone who did not follow their religious, man-made rules. Jesus described them as whitewashed tombs that were full of dead men's bones (Matt. 23:27). They were washed outside but filthy inside—clean but mean.

We see the same thing today. There's no doubt that most who attend a Sunday service are sincere people who love the Lord and want to grow spiritually. However, we have met church members whose negative and hateful attitudes would make a Pharisee look good. We have all met people who claim to be saved, but their words, attitude, and actions leave us wondering if they really have a relationship with Christ. Whatever they have is in their heads and not their hearts; in their lips and not their spirits (Mark 7:6).

Years ago we began a revival in January and it concluded eleven weeks later. A few weeks before the revival, Perry received a phone call from the pastor, informing him that he planned to leave the church and move to another city. Perry told him, "I'd rather not conduct a revival if the church is in the middle of contention and you are leaving. The strife can keep the Holy Spirit from ministering."

The pastor told Perry that he needed to come, because if the church did not experience revival, many would leave and it would become a divided congregation. We knew the meeting would be a challenge, but we accepted the invitation. Initially it was scheduled for only seven days.

The first week, a great flow of the Spirit hit the youth and many in the town began attending, being saved, and baptized in the Holy Spirit. This inspired the parents to attend, and soon grandparents were coming to experience what their grandchildren were talking about.

In the church were about eighty members who detested the pastor and wanted him out, and they were fearful that if the revival continued, the hearts of the members would change and this would cause the pastor to reverse his decision to leave. This group formed opposition teams that tried to end the revival in any way possible. Souls being converted met nothing to them. They cared only about their own selfish desires.

So many were being saved that one night, two hundred new members joined the church, much to the dismay of the eighty, who even called the church headquarters in Cleveland to try to have the revival shut down. Yet the services continued, the attendance grew, and the altars filled each night with people seeking more of God.

During the ninth week of the revival, Perry and I were in the pastor's office after the service. The associate pastor's wife came in and said, "There is a woman out here—she attends this church—and she is demanding to speak to you." We invited her in.

Immediately she began to shout that Perry was not of God; and if he were, these other people—that is, the ones resisting the revival—would be participating in the meeting. Perry (stirring things up again) reminded her that it is hard for a corpse to be resurrected once you've nailed the coffin lid shut. She railed on him in a manner I had never heard before.

My blood pressure was rising and I had listened to all the trash talk that I could handle. I jumped up and interrupted her, saying, "Who do you think you are, walking in this office and talking to my husband like this? He spends all day studying and praying for these services, and you don't know what you're talking about. I've told him, with the rotten attitude of some of these members who won't even attend the revival, we should pack up and get out of this town. Now shut your mouth and quit talking about my husband that way."

There was silence. I think she was stunned, since I'm normally a quiet person who minds my own business. But she had crossed the line into my territory. I knew my husband better than anyone else in that church, and he was preaching every night until he was exhausted. Later the woman apologized and sent a gift to our home following the meeting.

Another form of meanness was racism. Being from Alabama, I grew up in an area and a state that was once overflowing with racism. This form of hatred was falsely justified (sometimes in the name of God) by men who hid behind white robes, masks, and pointed hats.

When Perry's dad pastored a church in North Carolina, he preached a message against racism because he thought it was a problem that needed to be addressed. After the service, two men who were members of the church asked to speak privately with him. They threatened him, saying that if he ever spoke about racism being a sin, he would have to deal with them. That is when Fred learned that both men were members of the Ku Klux Klan.

Fred later said, "What former pastor in his right mind would have allowed these two spiritual reprobates to become members of the church?" Fred left that church—or maybe I should say, Fred was rescued from that church—and went to pastor a church in Hickory.

We held a revival at one church where some of the members wanted to close the meeting because people were parking on the grass and ruining it, and because people were using too much toilet paper. It stunned me that some people would be more concerned about grass and toilet paper than souls being saved.

Thankfully, there were far more churches that wanted revival and loved the new people. Those churches bought all the toilet paper that was needed! It was those churches that we would return to year after year, building relationships and watching converts grow in the faith.

People who have been Christians for many years can become set in their ways—especially in traditions that are not biblically-based, but culturally or denominationally-based. As we mature, we will either become hard-hearted or remain tender-hearted. We will become sweet or sour, cleaner or meaner. It is almost impossible to change a person who is bound up with a Pharisee spirit. But as a minister, you have to preach the Word and let the Lord do the rest.

CHAPTER 8

HEARING THE VOICE OF THE LORD

T HERE IS ONE area in which being married to a minister like Perry can be both a blessing and a challenge. No matter where we are, the Lord will give him an inspiration and he will suddenly be compelled to stop everything he is doing and write. Or sometimes an overwhelming burden hits him out of the blue, which is nearly always a warning of some kind.

Perry's dad always taught the importance of having an ear to hear the still, small voice of God at any moment of the day. If there was ever a man who could hear the voice of the Lord, it was Fred Stone. He would often come to the office to share with Perry some dream or word the Lord gave him, and those warnings turned out to be accurate. Perry used to say, "I wish dad could dream something good every now and then. He always gets a warning about something bad that's about to happen." Fred was like one of the Old Testament "seers" who acted as a watchman on the wall to bring God's warnings to people.

Through Fred's experiences, Perry learned how vital it is to have that kind of listening ear. As stated, Fred said that most Christians know how to speak to God, but they don't know how to listen to God. Just as Christ would do nothing except what he heard the Father tell Him, we must train our spirits and minds to hear and know the voice of God. That might come through an inward nudge or sudden impulse.

Or it might come through unmistakable instructions that flow to us from the Holy Spirit.

With Perry, he might have a dream or a vision. He might be shown somebody's need, or a battle they currently are facing or will be facing in the near future. The Lord might show him something about America or another nation. If he senses a burden, it might be a warning of impending danger, or some unforeseen circumstance that will hinder the ministry. When somebody close to us is on the verge of death, he will often sense a burden for that.

While it is a blessing that he hears from the Lord, it can be frustrating when this happens during family time—especially vacations. I don't let him take his laptop on vacation because it is vacation—not a time to study and write. But even without a laptop, if he gets a word from the Lord, he stops whatever he is doing and heads back to the hotel room to get a pen and paper. For years I chalked this up to being a workaholic. I thought he was addicted to studying. I said many times, "Can't you leave the studying alone for one week and take a vacation with the family?" He would reply, "I try. I really do try. But if I hear the Lord saying something, I can't tell Him to put it off until I get back. I have to write it down immediately."

If he gets a burden in the middle of some family activity, he becomes quiet, mopey, and disconnected. He has to go back to the room and pray, even if it means leaving me with our guests. It took me years to get accustomed to this. It took guests years to get accustomed to it, too.

I did learn, however, to pay attention when he finds himself dealing with one of these burdens. Years ago, we took a mini-vacation to the mountains of North Carolina, where we stayed in a beautiful log cabin and had no distractions. I was looking forward to a couple of days away, with just him and our daughter Amanda.

But late in the evening, he became overwhelmed in his spirit with a burden that became unbearable. Out of frustration I said to him, "Why do these burdens come on you during our vacations? Why can't we just have normal family time?"

Perry spent that evening in prayer and groaning intercession. The next morning he said, "I still don't know what this is about, but something is being planned today—some kind of attack by the enemy. We just need to be careful."

That morning we headed to Franklin, North Carolina and stopped in a gemstone shop that was also a museum for historic relics that had been discovered in the region. This place had two levels—an upper level that displayed the gemstones, with a ramp that led to the lower level where the artifacts were encased in large glass showcases. Perry was downstairs in a side room and I was viewing items in the showcase. Amanda was on the ramp behind me.

Suddenly Amanda ran down the ramp and was unable to stop her momentum. She tripped and fell right in front of a glass showcase. As she was falling, her momentum caused her to lunge face-first into the glass, hitting it so hard that I thought she would break the glass. Instead, she smashed her nose and it began to bleed profusely. The bleeding would not stop, and paramedics were called. It took about thirty minutes for her nose to stop bleeding.

Thank God she did not shatter the showcase glass with the force of her body and face. Only the Lord knows the injury it could have caused. Perry later said, "This is what the burden was about. She was protected from a situation that could have been far worse."

When these burdens come, I have learned to flow with them. The Holy Spirit is giving them for a reason.

While most husbands can take a vacation and spend the entire time focusing on the family and forgetting the cares of the workplace, it is hard for a man who lives in two worlds to do this. He is on duty twenty-four hours a day. He cannot shut his ear to the Holy Spirit, or take a vacation from burdens by saying, "Hold off on that until I return home."

A spiritual burden is a weight; it is heaviness in the spirit of the person who bears it. Sometimes this person has knowledge of a situation that brings a sense of spiritual urgency, and other times the person has no idea what this burden is about. Either way, it is important to pray. This could stop a terrible situation or a satanic attack.

Some burdens are gentle pressure to spend time with God. Others push a person toward deeper intercession and intimacy with God. Still other burdens are signals of impending danger or trouble, or a signal that a major transition is coming.

Perry also gets burdens that we have come to call a death burden. On about a dozen different occasions, a burden has settled over Perry that is different from others. This burden is a sign that someone close to us is about to pass from this life into eternity. Seven days before the death of one of our intercessors and close friends named Emie Piper, Perry was at the office; and as the morning passed, the weight became so heavy that he could no longer study. He said it feels like a depression. He told Gina, "I'm going home. I feel that death burden again." Seven days later Emie passed away at her home in Cleveland.

Gina Bean, who has been with the ministry thirteen years, has said, "I can tell when this death burden comes on Perry. He is disconnected, doesn't hear when you speak to him, and doesn't want to do any work that day. Eventually he will go home. When this burden comes on him, I know it means that within seven days, somebody will likely die."

One Saturday Perry was preparing to put down the top on his car and drive through the mountains, just to enjoy the day and clear his mind. As he was walking out the door, a heavy weight hit his spirit. He struggled with the idea of taking the drive. He began to pray in the Holy Spirit and received an interpretation: "If you go to the mountains today, there is an assignment of the enemy for you to be hit by a truck and killed in an accident." He stayed home.

On another Saturday, the same heaviness overcame him. He sensed that a premature death was coming, and he went to the prayer barn and prayed fervently for over an hour and a half, binding the spirit of death and speaking life. The burden lifted and he felt the Lord had heard his prayer.

Days later, our office manager's mother died, but she was revived by medical personnel. From a natural standpoint, she should have had irreversible physical damage. But we believe that the advanced warning and prayer halted the death spirit and kept her alive. She recovered and was able to return to work.

Four days later, VOE was hosting a mentoring school for ministry at the T.L. Lowery Global Foundation center in Cleveland. That was the same day that the tornado hit my hometown of Tuscaloosa, wiping out homes, neighborhoods, offices, and restaurants. Cleveland also suffered some damage from tornadoes that touched down throughout the day. But that night, as Perry was teaching, the news reported that there was a severe tornado watch for Bradley Country and the city of Cleveland. They said a funnel cloud was forming outside of Cleveland.

I called Perry while he was preaching and suggested he dismiss the people to go to their hotel rooms. He thought that might be too dangerous, but since we didn't know where the tornado might hit, anything could be a target for the F-4 tornado that was headed our way.

He told the people about the severe weather and called them to the front for immediate prayer. He went to the lobby and observed that dark clouds were forming in the distance, and the light fixture outside was swinging wildly. Wind was bouncing cars up and down in the parking lot. Perry cried out, "Lord, how do we pray right now?" The Holy Spirit said, "Command the tornado to split in half like the waters at the Red Sea."

Perry ran to the front and announced what he heard. Mark Casto took the microphone and began to fervently command the storm to split in half. One of the youth, Amanda Fisher, had a laptop and was watching the storm on satellite, as the tornado, unknown to us, was now over south Cleveland, ripping homes off their foundations.

Perry later reported that the people cried out to God with faith and energy, taking authority over the powers of the air and rebuking the storm. Within the hour, things were calm and settled. The following day, we learned that many homes were destroyed and a few people were even killed when this tornado struck.

We also learned that the F-4 was headed toward Michigan Avenue, in the direction of the homes of four of our staff and the two VOE office buildings. About three miles from the office, the tornado lifted part of a roof from a brick factory; then the storm split in half. One half took out a small neighborhood and caused much damage to one section of Cleveland. The other half died down. At the office the only damage was to an awning. Everyone at the conference was safe, with no damage to their cars.

I cannot explain why some homes were destroyed and others were not, or why some were killed when others were spared. I do believe, however, that the Saturday intercession spared the people at the conference, the ministry center, and the homes of the staff.

A spiritual burden is difficult to carry day after day, and it can be lifted only through fervent prayer and intense intercession. Fred Stone taught that, when an unusual burden rests upon you, immediately find a place to pray, and pray until you feel relief. The sense of relief and inner peace is the indicator that God has heard, the situation is covered, and He will intervene.

These spiritual burdens might explain one of the keys to the success of Perry's ministry. He would become burdened for the churches where he preached, burdened for a revival to break out, burdened to see results in the altars, and burdened to see needs met. Burdens led him to hours of prayer. Then when he preached that night, the anointing of the Holy Spirit would lead to results in the altars. Sometimes hundreds of people in one revival would be saved and filled with the baptism of the Holy Spirit. At times the entire town would be impacted by the revival.

Spiritual results are birthed out of spiritual travail. It is possible that our altars in America's churches are barren because not enough people are in spiritual labor giving birth to converts. When Zion travailed, she brought forth her children (Isaiah 66:8).

I don't have that same kind of ear that Perry has, but I do have that "gut feeling" when something is not right. I am not much of a dreamer, but the few times that I dream, it generally means something. Many years ago I dreamed that one of our best friends in the ministry suffered a severe attack from the enemy. I picked up Perry from the airport and asked if we could drop by the minister's church on a Wednesday night. We spent the night with them and discovered that the dream dealt with something that had occurred. The Lord brought assurance to the couple that all would be fine. Today they have a powerful and growing ministry that impacts the world.

We often say it is a woman's intuition that is directing her. But I believe it is more than that. I believe it is the Holy Spirit speaking to our spirits and giving us warning or direction. When I begin to sense certain thoughts, they are generally correct. This gift could be called discernment. It is a powerful gift for a wife that also helps protect her husband and children from people who might have wrong intentions.

PROTECTION BY ANGELS

If you are a partner of the ministry or have listened to Perry preach for any length of time, you might have heard him tell of two occasions in which he saw an angel of the Lord. When he was eighteen, he saw one during an altar service at the Church of God Camp meeting in the open air tabernacle. He was on the left side of the altar praying when suddenly he saw a large figure of a man, transparent in appearance, with a white radiance, and he walked through the wall. Great fear overwhelmed Perry and he fell to his knees in a hiding position.

The second encounter was in Romania, when he and Jentezen Franklin were there preaching. At three o'clock in the morning, an angelic being entered their room, causing the entire room to light up. Both he and Jentezen said they could feel this angel's presence so strongly that their hair stood straight up.

I have never seen an angel; nor, as far as I know, have I encountered one that would appear in the form of a stranger, such as appeared to Lot in Genesis 19. However, I am convinced there have been times when an angel of the Lord has been assigned to protect someone in my family. Perry's dad told stories of how God sent an angel to speak to a person and give instructions for their protection.

The life of my own mother was spared from premature death when the tornado struck Tuscaloosa, Alabama a couple of years ago. For the past several years my mother, who lives in Tuscaloosa, has come to Cleveland to stay with us for about six weeks in the spring. In April of 2011, she had just arrived at our home when the terrible storms struck the Southeastern United States. They began on April 25 and continued through the 28th. There was a rash of tornadoes in twenty-one states, with the southern states getting the brunt of the destruction. By the time they ended, 348 people had been killed.

On April 27, a massive tornado twisted through my hometown of Tuscaloosa. A women I call Aunt Bobbie is a close family friend who was in her home when the storm struck. Aunt Bobbie was crouched in the hallway holding onto a pillow when the twister hit her home, blowing everything in the house away and leaving only the stairs in the house intact. The strong winds picked her up and blew her fifty feet away, where she was found lying under a wall that landed on top of her. Neighbors heard her screaming and removed the wall, then carried her to safety on a door that had been blown off its hinges.

Aunt Bobbie's survival was a miracle that is also connected to my mother. I had asked Mom to come to Cleveland a little earlier than normal because of our schedule and she agreed. For years, when a storm came through the Tuscaloosa-Northport area, my mother would immediately go to Aunt Bobbie's house to ride out the storm or to seek cover. Had I not picked up Mom earlier than usual, she would have been in town at that very house when the tornado ripped the home to pieces. My mother could have died or been seriously injured in the storm. But thankfully, she was safe with us.

One remarkable story comes from Charlie Ellis. In April of 1999, his sister Jana was preparing for marriage and she and her fiancé, Jeremy Reid, found a house and were closing on it prior to the August marriage. They had saved money for over a year and found a perfect starter home. Because the house was in a rural area where there was a volunteer fire department, the department required proof that the local fire dues were paid before they could close on the house. The day before they were to close and pay the fire dues, their broker called and informed them that they needed an additional $400 for closing the next day.

They did not have the money and their parents were not able to assist. Jana prayed and told the Lord that she knew this was to be their house and that, somehow, she would pay the fire dues and the Lord would just have to work it out on their behalf. The fire station told her they needed the number from a plaque that was posted on a tree in the yard, because that number would be used to verify that the property owner had paid the bill.

Jana drove to the house and was standing in the front yard looking at the plaque, when suddenly a man pulled in the driveway. He stepped out of his car and walked toward her and said, "The Lord told me to give you this." He pulled a large amount of cash from his pocket and handed it to her. Before she could respond, he was back in his car and had pulled out of the driveway. She immediately got in her car to follow him. As he drove around the curve, it was as though he simply disappeared. She looked for him and could find neither him nor the car.

When she counted the money, she discovered twenty $20 bills. Only her family knew that they needed the money, so she joyfully headed to her parent's house to tell her mother about this unusual answer to prayer. As she entered the house, she passed a picture of her grandparents on the mantle—the same picture she had passed many times over the years. This time she stopped in her tracks and realized that the man in the picture was the same man who handed her the money. He looked just like her grandfather, Charles Ellis, who had died ten years before she was born. She never personally knew either of her grandparents, but the look was unmistakably identical.

To this day Jana says she cannot understand how God did this and does not know who this person actually was. But to her, this was a messenger of the Lord who brought her a financial miracle at the very moment she needed it.

We know that angels can appear in human form, at times as strangers unaware (Heb. 13:2). And while her grandfather was a Christian who died in relationship with the Lord, this was most likely an angelic being that took on the form of a person and the appearance of someone recognizable.

Before we were married, Perry was scheduled to preach a revival in Jackson, Mississippi. He had driven from Virginia to Northport where he spent the night at Charlotte and Jerry's house to break up the long trip. He left early Sunday morning for the drive to Mississippi. He was tired when he left before dark, but he knew he must stay alert.

About thirty minutes into the drive, he started getting sleepy along a stretch of interstate highway that was, at that time, a long and boring drive with few exits or places to stop. Rolling down the window and playing music did not keep him awake, and he fell asleep. He was drifting off the left lane onto the side, with the cruise set at 65 miles-per-hour. Suddenly he felt a hand strike him in the back between the shoulder blades, thrusting his body forward toward the steering wheel. He saw the danger and immediately moved back into the lane. He had been headed toward the corner of an interstate bridge, where within moments he would have crashed into the abutment.

The burning feeling of a hand remained pressed upon him for a few minutes, and he was absolutely confident that the Lord had sent an angel to protect him from death or a disabling accident on the highway.

Many people were familiar with the many stories Perry's dad shared with audiences to illustrate the supernatural power of God in his life and ministry. On several occasions, Fred saw in a dream or a vision a supernatural being he knew was an angel of the Lord. On at least two occasions, the Holy Spirit gave him instructions to ask God to send an angel to go forth and protect an individual whose life was in danger.

In the Bible, when Peter was imprisoned and scheduled for beheading the following morning, the saints prayed all night and God sent an angel to release Peter from prison. When Peter arrived at the house, the prayer meeting was still going on. Peter knocked on the door so someone would let him in the house. A young woman heard his voice and announced that Peter was outside. But the prayer warriors must not have believed what they were praying for, because one person said:

"And as Peter knocked at the door of the gate, a girl named Rhoda came to answer. When she recognized Peter's voice, because of her gladness she did not open the gate, but ran in and announced that Peter stood before the gate. But they said to her, "You are beside yourself!" Yet she kept insisting that it was so. So they said, "It is his angel."
– Acts 12:13-15 (NKJV)

When those praying said, "It is his angel," this could mean they believed it was the personal guardian angel of Peter that had arrived at the door. When Jesus was speaking about God's love for children, He taught that in heaven the angels that are assigned to these children behold the face of God continually (Matt. 18:10). There appear to be angels assigned to individuals or, in some cases, entire families or clans. Jacob spoke about an angel that redeemed him and went with him on his journeys, and he asked the same angel to be with his grandchildren:

> *"The Angel who has redeemed me from all evil, bless the lads; let my name be named upon them, and the name of my fathers Abraham and Isaac; And let them grow into a multitude in the midst of the earth."*
> *– Genesis 48:16 (NKJV)*

Angels are heavenly beings that are given earthly assignments. The angel of the Lord encamps around those that fear Him, and delivers them (Psalm 34:6-8). To encamp means to pitch a tent or to rest in a tent, indicating that angels actually camp out in places where men and women dwell who are in covenant with God. Job was protected from Satan's attacks by a hedge that could not be penetrated. This protective hedge may have been angels that kept watch over Job, his family, and his possessions.

When God blesses you with children, they move from the innocent childhood years to the challenging teen years. With sinful vices such as alcohol, drugs and pornography, danger lurks in their path. Premature death traps are concealed by normal looking surroundings. As parents, we are not always with them, so prayer is necessary to form an invisible hedge around them. Job, a man of integrity, had a hedge encircling him, his children, and their homes. Only when God gave Satan permission was the enemy able to pierce the hedge.

As righteous parents, we must continually pray to keep our children under our covering and hedge. This is the prayer we pray, and it is a prayer that Perry's father prayed the moment his first child was born. He prayed: "Lord, I pray that you will protect my family, and keep them from harm, danger, and disabling accidents."

We must keep our blood line secure under the protective promises of God, and one of those promises is that angels are assigned to the believer (Ps. 34:6-8).

PART THREE

MANNA-FEST AND BEYOND

An early picture of the Taylor family—my parents, my sisters, and me. I'm on the far left.

The Perry Stone I first met

Wedding day, April 2, 1982

The dedication of our first purchased office building. Jonathan was just a few weeks old.

Perry and Charlie Ellis in one of the first offices we had outside our home

My first job as the VOE product salesperson, 1986

First time being baptized in the Jordan River

Aunt Gladys, who took my sisters and me to church

My best friend, Tracy Davis, who was killed in a tragic car accident in 1990

Enjoying our first cruise

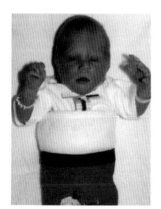

Jonathan Gabriel Stone, born December 23, 1989, when we brought him home from the hospital in a Christmas stocking

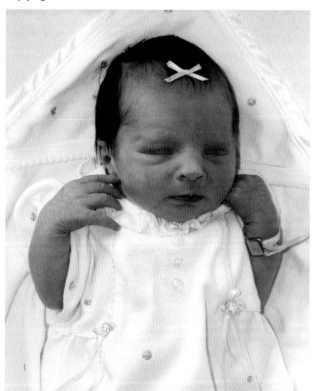

Amanda Michelle Stone, born August 1, 2001

Taken during a baby shower given by Daughter's of Rachel when I was pregnant with Amanda

Pastor Howard Hancock and his wife Naomi at the Baltimore Harbor, helping to keep Perry "balanced."

At Grandma and Grandpa Bava's house in Davis, West Virginia

The Stone family, taken at Fred and Juanita's 50th anniversary celebration

My niece standing in Aunt Bobbie's yard after the tornado in Tuscaloosa, Alabama

Jonathan with NBA star and VOE partner, Lawrence Funderburke

My oldest sister Shelia and her family—Jeff, Jake, and Jordan Branham

Guess which team we're rooting for?

Getting ready to watch the big game—National Championship between Alabama and LSU

Visiting the Greenbrier in White Sulphur Springs, West Virginia

Amanda and I with Ruby Gettinger, from the Ruby Show

Jonathan's 21st birthday

Jonathan loves his little sister, Amanda!

Enjoying a meal with Perry's parents, Fred and Juanita, and Lewis and Glenda Mason

Rev. Perry Fred Stone, Sr. and wife Juanita, three years before Fred passed away. Love my in-laws!

Playing in the mud at the Dead Sea (that's Perry, second from left)

Amanda's first trip to Israel

Sitting at the covered bridge on the Omega Ranch property

Mom and I

The Taylor sisters

My sister Shelia and I, in a boat on the Sea of Galilee

Having fun with Rick and Karen Wheaton Towe

Perry and I with Kendra and Phil Stacey at the Hope House fundraiser, A Night of Hope

Jerry and Charlotte Skelton (center, front and back) and their family. This is the family I lived with when I met Perry.

My youngest sister Carla and her husband Rusty Pate, with Luke and Lindsay Pate, Scotty and Jessica Pate, and Lindsey and Alan Martin on their wedding day

The family being baptized in the Jordan River

Taken at Gideon Springs in Israel, with Gideon Shor, who has been our tour guide since 1985

My surprise 50th birthday party

Jonathan's graduation from college

Mom and I as we enjoy watching our favorite team play football

Flying to one of the conferences

Precious volunteers during our annual Partner's Conference in Pigeon Forge, Tennessee

Trip to Israel at the remains of Nimrod's fortress in the Golan Heights

Two of my blessings in life—my mother Stella Taylor and my mother-in-law Juanita Stone

Working in the garden

The kitchen on the farm

Connie Herring and ladies from Women of Hope, in the farm kitchen with veggies from the garden

OCI groundbreaking ceremony

Perry and I with some of the OCI family

THE INSIDE STORY
OF MANNA-FEST

OUR MINISTRY PARTNERS have heard this story many times, but to me it never gets old because the birth of Manna-fest was a Divine directive from the Lord. But I would like share the details as I remember them.

The story begins in Florida where we were conducting a revival at Zephyrhills Church of God. When we arrived we learned that Pastor Tom Jammes had felt impressed to contact Arthlene Rippy, director of "The Good Life," a daily program aired live on CTN (Christian Television Network) out of Clearwater, Florida. Pastor Tom asked the host to interview Perry and discuss recent prophetic events, since communism was beginning to collapse in Poland and parts of Eastern Europe, and many Americans had questions that they wanted answered. Not knowing Perry, the host was hesitant, but decided to give him a one-hour interview.

When the phones were opened and people were allowed to ask questions, his interview was said to generate one of the best responses in some time. Perry felt comfortable before a camera and spoke as though he were in your home, sitting across the table from you. One man who had worked with a major television ministry commented that, after watching Perry and being with him in the studio, he believed that Perry had a gift for television ministry.

That day while driving back from the studio, Pastor Tom told Perry that this was the beginning of something new for him and television would be part of the ministry. Pastor said, "The day will come when your attendance will be so large that you will not be able to come to my church, because you will not be able to hold the people."

That December 1989 interview was a tiny opening that would one day lead to a global ministry. But the unique part of this story was a visitation from the Lord that occurred a year earlier at the same church. We were staying in the pastor's home, and on the six o'clock news was a breaking story that involved a well-known evangelist and an alleged moral indiscretion. None of us could believe what we were hearing.

We were close friends with the daughter and son-in-law of a family who served on that minister's board of directors. We assumed the press was attacking the minister with a false report and we were concerned that many people would see this and become despondent or angry. Perry called our friend and asked if he had heard this televised report. To his dismay the man replied, "Yes. My father-in-law just received a phone call from the minister who told him there was a story coming out."

That night the church was packed, but the hearts of the people were sad and confused. Perry preached, and when we returned to the pastor's home that night, more details were being released. We were all heartbroken. We also were concerned about how this would impact the faith and confidence of millions of believers, and even sinners who admired this man's ministry. After watching the news that night, Perry and the pastor felt they should return to the church and pray. I was not in that prayer meeting, but I have heard Perry relay the events many times.

Both men were in deep travail, praying for the body of believers and the minister and his family. They interceded for a long time because they did not know the extent of the damage this man's failure would cause around the world. They knew mockers and scoffers would have a heyday with this report, because this man was known for his sermons against sin.

Finally, tiredness set in, and Perry decided to lie down on the front pew with a Bible under his head. He was not asleep, but in a condition where he was half here and half in the Spirit realm. It was about three o'clock in the morning.

Suddenly, in his ear he heard a clear voice say, "Manna-Fest." The word normally would be spelled manifest, meaning something unknown that is made visible or known. However, he heard M-A-N-N-A – F-E-S-T. He opened his eyes and sat up thinking, "Wow, I have never heard that name before! What is that about?" He then clearly heard a follow-up statement in his ear saying, "This will be the title of the television program I am giving you." He laughed and said in his mind, "I am definitely not interested in a television program."

When he returned home early in the morning, he slept a few hours and told me the next day, "I have something to tell you, but you have to keep it secret." When he told me what happened and that he was given the name "Manna-fest," I knew this was from the Lord, even though Perry had no interest in television. At the time we didn't even own a video camera, much less television equipment or a studio.

It reminds me of the story of Abraham and Isaac. Abraham was seventy-five when God spoke to him about his future son, and how this son would make a great nation. But twenty-four years later, his wife Sarah was still barren, Abraham was ninety-nine years old, and the promise had not come to pass. But when Abraham was one hundred years old, Isaac was born through the barren womb of Sarah.

The Bible tells us that God calls those things that are not as though they were (Rom. 4:17). Long before a promise is fulfilled, the Lord speaks to us as though it already exists, for in God's mind, it has already been planned. Through a divine vision God gives us the ability to see the future before the project ever begins. The Lord only gives us bits and pieces of the puzzle of destiny, as a full revelation might frighten us and make us feel we could not fulfill the assignment. We have to act upon what has been revealed, and through obedience, the entire puzzle will come together.

From the time the name Manna-fest was revealed to the time the first program was aired was about twelve years. When the time arrived, the team was in place, the equipment purchased, and the airtime paid for. Now Manna-fest is on the air in North America and about 250 nations around the world.

According to Nielsen Ratings, Manna-fest is often rated among the top three programs on Christian television. The Russian Manna-fest telecast is the third most-watched program on Russian Christian television. Letters and e-mails pour in from around the world with testimonies of conversions to Christ, deliverance from bondages, restoration of marriages, and other blessings received after hearing the Word preached on the Manna-fest program.

THE PROPHETIC MESSAGE WAS BIRTHED

Over the years we have learned that God will align events, people, and circumstances in ways that you cannot imagine at the time. But suddenly, like a puzzle, all the pieces come together to form a perfect picture. This is what happened with the Manna-fest program.

We took our first tour of the Holy Land in May of 1985. We had never been outside of the United States, and on this first trip we took 120 people, mostly close friends. We fell in love with Israel, and Perry was intrigued with the wealth of information he was gleaning from our tour guide, Gideon Shor. He learned about the large vultures that were populating the Golan Heights, which is an area where future wars of prophecy will be fought (Ezek. 38-39). Through Gideon and his brother-in-law who lived in Tel-Aviv, Perry learned of an earthquake fault line running across the Mount of Olives into Jerusalem, which is the very mountain that will split when Christ returns (Zech. 14:4).

The following year we hosted a second trip, and about 180 people made the pilgrimage. On this trip, a photographer documented the tour using slide film. We returned home with hundreds of beautiful slides. This is when Perry had an idea. He saw the slides and thought, "Would it be possible to preach with a slide projector and show these places in Israel during the message?" The only way to know how successful this would be was to test it with a prophetic message. He began to work on a message that he titled, "Inside Israel Update," which included pictures flashed on the screen to authenticate the information.

One of his first and most unusual messages was called, "The Ashes of the Red Heifer." This message explained the ancient ritual of offering a burnt red heifer and mixing the ashes to purify the unclean. In Israel we learned that, in order to rebuild a Jewish Temple, they would need a red heifer. The heifer would be burned and the ashen water sprinkled on the building and the reconstructed furniture. This subject became his most popular prophecy update, and was eventually taught using slides from Israel.

In each revival, the Saturday night service was designated Prophecy Update Night. This became the most interesting and well-attended service of the week. Many of the older prophetic ministers had used charts to illustrate timelines and events, but this was a new method for Perry. The fact that the biblical information was confirmed by pictures caused people's eyes to be opened, and unsaved people began to respond to the altar calls. We found that people who never attended church were more likely to attend on Saturday night, as they viewed this as more of a news documentary than a church service.

The challenge to this type of teaching was that people in the back of the church could not always see the places being pointed out on the screen. After the service, people came to me at our resource table and suggested that we put the information on a video. But Perry questioned, "How can I do that? We don't own any equipment to do that sort of thing." As always, God already had that arranged.

Highland Hills, the church in Lenoir City, Tennessee, had a television ministry. The pastor allowed Perry to work with the television team to produce several prophetic videos. He sat in a chair with his notes on his lap and a slide projector remote control in his hand. Two cameras were set up—one for him to speak into and another for flashing the slides onto a screen. He would teach and change slides, as the producer switched from Perry to the slides, and then back to Perry. In one day, he taped for eight hours, which produced four videos. Today technology has improved and editing equipment can place pictures and scriptures directly onto the taped session. But in those days, everything had to be done the long and hard way.

After editing hundreds of scriptures on four videos, Charlie Ellis discovered that the scripture references had so many misspelled words that we lost count. But those videos, as primitive as they seem today, helped launch the ministry onto television.

CHRISTIAN TELEVISION

Neither of us had any idea how God would orchestrate and birth a television program, and no doors were opening for that kind of ministry. However, in the early 1990s, Perry received an important phone call that would later set the course for God's will. A Christian station, CTN in Tampa, the same station that aired the interview in 1989, called and asked Perry to assist them in their yearly telethon. At first he was hesitant because he is uncomfortable asking for money, even for our own ministry. We hear so many Christians complain that ministers are too focused on money and are always asking for offerings, even though ministry cannot be run without funds. But the station asked him to teach on the subject of Bible prophecy, and they wondered if he had any prophetic resources that could be offered as a gift to those donating to the station.

At that time we had the four prophetic videos that we offered on our resource table during revivals. CTN committed to enact an idea they had never done before. They chose to offer the four videos with eight hours of teaching, along with a cassette message, to those who would support the network with a donation of a specific amount. This would be a blessing for Perry, because it would allow him to minister live for several hours on a Christian television network, and reach cities where we had never traveled and ministered.

That night, there were not enough phones to answer the calls for the videos. The success of the telethon and the spiritual results of people being touched by the message spread throughout the Christian network world, and soon other networks were calling Perry to come to their station and teach the prophetic message. The stations would usually offer one or more of the videos.

Through these appearances over several years, the Voice of Evangelism was able to purchase their own television equipment in

1994. By the time we were in the 7,500 square-foot office building, God had blessed us with cameras and the equipment required to create a quality video resource.

It was clear that the yearly Israel tours continually stroked Perry's fire of prophetic interest. On each new trip, it seemed that there was a new discovery, a prophetic link to a location, and specific places where the words of biblical prophets were being fulfilled. These were documented in slides and photographs, and eventually on small hand-held video recorders. The quality of the videos in those days was not even close to what we see today in our present studio, but it was a start.

In 1999, Charlie Ellis and Perry went to Monroe, Louisiana for a telethon. While a guest musician was singing, Perry asked Charles Reed, the owner of the station, about the possibility of airing a television program on the network. Charles, a great man of faith, instantly agreed. Perry then did a live survey on the station and asked the audience how many would watch a weekly program if he had one. The response was positive as calls poured in for about thirty minutes. For the first time, since hearing the words Manna-fest eleven years earlier, a seed was planted to begin a weekly telecast.

The fall months arrived and the Main Event, which is still our primary yearly conference, was in progress. The Saturday night service took a turn about halfway into the worship. A member of the ministry team suddenly began to speak a prophetic word over the ministry and over Perry, saying that it was time to begin a television program that would reach the world. This word led to another and yet another confirmation. It was clear, by revelation of the Holy Spirit, that the time had arrived for the word that God gave years earlier about Manna-fest to be fulfilled.

Charlie Ellis began to contact stations and discuss possible air time. Perry had been a guest on enough Christian stations to establish a reputation as a prophetic teacher and to already have an audience that desired to hear more of this type of teaching on a regular basis. After several months of planning and taping programs from the studio, Manna-fest aired for the first time on the station in Monroe, Louisiana on Friday, September 1, 2000.

During the first year, most of the programs were taped from our studio. But people really wanted to see on-location teaching from Israel, which required two special cameras. In November of 2000, two cameras, including one purchased by our ministry partner Emie Piper, were taken on the tour. Perry and the crew began taping 24-minute television programs, teaching Hebraic-prophetic insight. Within months of airing the Israel programs, we knew why God had called Perry into the television ministry. Within several years, some Christian stations said this was one of their top-viewed programs.

Each month the ministry receives hundreds of testimonies and praise reports from families in the U.S., individuals in foreign nations, and men who are incarcerated, telling us they either converted to Christ or rededicated their lives after watching Manna-fest. The Director of TBN Russia met with Perry in Israel and said that the Manna-fest program, which is translated into the Russian language, is the third most watched program on the network in Russia. Their station receives as many as 30,000 e-mails each day, and people speak of what they are learning and how they are impacted by the programming. The Russian version of Manna-fest is also aired in Israel, giving over a million Russian-speaking Jews access to the knowledge of the Messiah! The TBN Director showed Perry one e-mail from a Jewish girl in Israel who said that, after viewing the weekly program for several months, she had received Christ as her Messiah and Savior.

A few years ago Gina Bean received a phone call from a woman in the northeast who was from a Spirit-filled Catholic background. Her husband was a successful Jewish attorney, and she had witnessed to him for many years, to no avail. She was watching a Manna-fest program where Perry was speaking about future wars in Israel. She called her husband into the room by saying, "War is coming to Israel." He began watching the program. Two years later, he accepted Christ and became a believer.

In many nations where U.S. troops are stationed, Manna-fest has been one of the most viewed programs because of its prophetic emphasis and the programs filmed from Israel. The program is watched by Muslims for the same reason—they are also interested in prophecy, and they watch to view the various locations and places in Israel (which they call Palestine). One Indonesian businessman was staying in an expensive hotel in Dubai when he saw the program on the hotel television.

We also receive a tremendous response from men who are incarcerated. Each month we receive mail from men who have received salvation and deliverance after watching Manna-fest or reading some of the many books that the ministry has sent to prisons around the country. The ministry has received letters from incarcerated men who converted from Nation of Islam after reading *Unleashing the Beast*.

The word of the Lord that came concerning Manna-fest in February 1988, and the vision of a man standing at the television tower in July 1988, have been confirmed as the weekly telecast reaches around the world. Through satellite, cable and the internet, Perry preaches somewhere in the world every day. In the Bible, manna was the supernatural bread sent down from heaven during Israel's wandering in the wilderness. Fest is short for festival. Thus, Manna-fest speaks of a fresh word from God and a celebration in the Word and Spirit. It was a name given by God, and it is our spiritual inheritance. Several ministers have told Perry that the name Manna-fest is one of the best names of any program on Christian television. He reminds them that it was not his idea; it was revealed to him by the Lord during a late-night prayer meeting.

We and our partner's believe that the Manna-fest telecast was a plan in the mind of God long before there was ever television, cable, satellite or Perry Stone. The tours to Israel and the love for the Hebraic roots of our faith were all birthed in Perry's spirit by the Lord Himself. God has directed our steps through seasons of opposition, persecution and misunderstanding, to bring us to a place of international recognition in the Body of Christ. To God we give all the glory!

LIVING DEBT FREE

Partners who are familiar with our ministry are aware that Perry moves forward in any ministry project with the intent of the project being completed debt free. This can be a challenge, because we don't send fund raising letters to a mailing list asking for contributions.

When you don't ask, people assume you don't need provision. But the level of finances required for global evangelism reaches millions of dollars each year, just for television airtime. From the beginning, we have been led by three Scriptures for all we do:

> *"Not slothful in business; fervent in spirit; serving the Lord."*
> *- Romans 12:11 (KJV)*

> *"For which of you, intending to build a tower, does not sit down first and count the cost, whether he has enough to finish it, lest, after he has laid the foundation, and is not able to finish, all who see it begin to mock him, saying, 'This man began to build and was not able to finish.'"* *- Luke 14:28-30 (NKJV)*

> *"Owe no man anything, but to love one another: for he that loves another hath fulfilled the law."* *- Romans 13:8 (KJV)*

The reason for no debt is because the borrower becomes a servant to the lender (Proverbs 22:7). When heavy debt is incurred in ministry, the weight of paying it falls upon the leader of the ministry, and this can blur his or her focus. Instead of concentrating upon the Word of God, the emphasis is on paying the bills each month. Even an anointed minister can become chained to debt, and consequently become fearful of preaching messages that could offend large donors or cause some to leave the church. So when we begin a major building project or a new outreach, we do so with a debt-free mindset.

We also want our personal lives to operate debt free. When we bought our first house, we did not own a washer or dryer. Perry would not buy these on credit, so we had to wait several months until we could afford to buy them. We saved until we could pay cash. There are two things we have financed—a vehicle and our home.

I did convince him years ago to let me buy a Rainbow vacuum cleaner and make payments. It was a great vacuum cleaner until he decided to use it to clean the carpets in the office. He did not put enough water in the container, which burned up the motor. That was the end of his janitorial days. We decided he should stick to preaching and leave the cleaning for someone else.

Remaining debt free requires that we plan in advance, save money, and avoid credit card debt. For the ministry to maintain a debt free flow requires consistent and steady financial support from partners and individuals who are blessed by the ministry and trust us with their support. We are careful with ministry money and don't waste it. We save everywhere we can and purchase equipment only as needed.

Sometimes Perry preaches something that people disagree with, and they withdraw financial giving to the ministry. This comes with the territory. Even Jesus preached and ran off the entire congregation one time, leaving his disciples on the front row looking at one another. When this happens, we have to keep moving forward. We cannot allow negative opinions to influence or change our vision and assignment.

We are able to operate debt free because of the many materials we sell at revivals, conferences, and on the Manna-fest program. But without our many supportive partners and friends of the ministry, the ministry would not be where it is today. Perry's first ministry partners were his family—his parents, his Aunts Janet, Millie and Caroline, his grandparents John and Lucy Bava, and Bill and Nalvie Stone. These were his first cassette tape message partners with the Tape of the Month Club. Since those messages, which were taped all the way back to 1979, hundreds of thousands of cassette and CD messages have been heard by tens of thousands of partners.

Without our partners, we would be limited in the number of souls we could reach around the world. Without personal discipline, we would be under needless pressure to pay a mountain of debt. It is a relief to "owe no man nothing, but to love him."

I WANT TO KNOW ABOUT YOUR MONEY

One November we were ministering at a conference in Cartersville, Georgia at the Church at Liberty Square—a great congregation pastored by our long term friend, Joe Edwards, who also presided over our wedding. The pastor asked if Perry would be willing to go to the children's church and allow the children, aged five to ten, to ask any question they wanted. He obliged.

Well, you know how children have great imaginations and can occasionally ask some embarrassing questions or make embarrassing comments.

One question dealt with the kind of foods we will eat in heaven. Another concerned the possibility of gold commodes there. On the heels of that question, someone asked, "Will we have to use the bathroom in a resurrected body?" Suddenly another young man shot up his hand. Perry pointed to him and the boy stood and boldly asked, "Are you rich?" Perry laughed and said, "Did your mom or dad tell you to ask that question?"

Money and finances are the number one subjects that people are interested in when it comes to ministry. If the minister has a secular job or outside income, people don't question this much. But if his paycheck comes from tithes and offerings, people want to know how much he makes and how he spends it.

In our case, some of Perry's income is from sources outside of Voice of Evangelism. He has written songs that pay royalties, and he receives book advances from a Christian publisher to write books for them to publish and distribute. However, he has never taken money from the sale of any audio or printed resource—tape, video, DVD, CD or book that is sold through the ministry—whether in conferences, over the Internet, at the office, through book stores, or any other source. All income generated from the sale of teaching and resource material is put entirely into the Voice of Evangelism ministry.

When Perry preaches in conferences and other services, unless the offering is publicly designated toward something else, all of it goes directly into the Voice of Evangelism. Perry has spent most Thursdays in the fall and spring mentoring people for ministry, and he does not charge or get paid for this. He directs the OCI ministry and preaches there once a month, but has never been paid for doing so. Everything he does is part of ministry and obedience to God.

From the late 1980s to early 1990s, we showed our ministry income and expenses to the partners at the annual banquet in Pigeon Forge at the Grand Hotel. At that time and for many years, Perry's salary through the Voice of Evangelism was $18,000 a year. When people asked how we lived off that amount, he pointed out that we stayed (at that time) on the road over 250 days a year and the local churches provided our lodging and meals during those days. We were seldom home. The ministry's Board of Directors voted to provide us with a housing allowance, insurance, and a travel allowance while we were on the road. This was over and above the salary. At that time the ministry also paid me a salary of about $10,000 a year, so between all of that, all of our needs were met.

In the late 1990s, a CPA suggested to the Board of Directors that, with the growth of the ministry, Perry's salary should increase. The CPA said that the IRS would question a salary that low when the ministry was growing. With a 501(c)3, salaries are not permitted to be either too low or too high. We knew of one minister who was accused of taking a salary that was too high. The rules of the IRS can be complicated, and it is important to work with people who know what they're doing and can provide accurate direction.

There is no question that some ministers have manipulated ministry or church members for their own financial benefit. They have emphasized an unbalanced message of prosperity or used the sincerity of the giving of offerings to make outlandish promises to the giver. Sometimes there is no biblical basis for what they are saying, but it simply tickles the ears of the giver. Thankfully, most ministers are not like this.

This is an area where Perry made a commitment from the time of his youth. He said that he would not place an emphasis on money, but would allow the Spirit of God to speak to the people about the amount of money they should give. All of our major purchases, from land to paying for the last three buildings, have been paid for by praying in the needed income, and the Lord leads people to give toward the project.

Voice of Evangelism will also never sell any names on our mailing list. Companies will purchase names from different organizations so they can offer their products for sale, but we consider these names a sacred trust. The ministry does not send out donor letters asking for support. We do, however, have partners who support the ministry, and their support provides money for things such as employee salaries, property, television airtime, and audio or television equipment. We are thankful that God speaks to people to give when the finances are needed.

FROM DUCT TAPE TO KING AIR

Several years ago the Voice of Evangelism purchased an eight-seat twin engine plane for the ministry, so Perry and the team can have quick transportation to the churches where he ministers. Some people demand to know why a ministry needs a plane, but those who criticize are those who stay in one place and seldom travel.

The decision to do this came years ago, when Perry was so exhausted from long drives or long airport delays and plane changes that he was thinking about cancelling speaking engagements. On one occasion he missed a speaking engagement because the plane was having mechanical problems. When he returned to Chattanooga through Atlanta, he counted at least thirty different planes that were having mechanical difficulties that had caused hours of delays. When no planes were flying from Atlanta to Chattanooga, he had to get ground transportation back home. He spoke to another minister, Karen Wheaton, about this who told him, "If you don't get a plane to get yourself in and out faster, you'll burn out and lose your desire to travel. That is what happened to me."

We had an experienced pilot at our home church, and he began to fly Perry in a rented plane. He could leave in the afternoon and be home by midnight most of the time. It was so convenient and easy that the Board of Directors voted to purchase a plane, which is today a King Air F-90 that seats eight people, including the pilot. This has enabled Perry to go from Cleveland to Chicago, to Atlanta, to Dallas, and to Orlando to speak—all in seven days. With ground or commercial air transportation, this would have been costly, tiring, and probably impossible.

With a plane, seven team members can fly to a city and be back that night. This costs much less than it would to fly this many people commercially in the middle of the week, and we don't have to pay for hotel rooms for the night.

We both believe that God blesses those who seek first His kingdom (Matt. 6:33). Christ said that if we give, then it will be given to us, with the same measure that we use (Luke 6:38).

When we purchase anything for our personal use, we must pay for it personally. That is an IRS rule for ministries, and you will be in trouble if you don't follow it. We are not permitted to take money from ministry funds and purchase clothes, furniture, or vehicles for personal use. Yet, we have three vehicles that the Lord provided for us. One of those was a Hummer that was given to Perry several years ago by a ministry friend in Louisiana. This has proven to be a blessing on the OCI property where some of the terrain is still rough.

Sometimes people become angry that we would spend "ministry money" on such a vehicle. This is what happens when people don't know us personally and don't know that the Hummer was a gift that cost us nothing. One woman saw me driving the Hummer and commented, "I see where Perry Stone is spending poor people's money on an expensive vehicle." She was ignorant of the facts, yet was willing to consider her ignorance of facts as the truth. What do we do in situations like this?

My philosophy, after all these years, is to stop wasting time responding to the critics. They will never accept your explanation, anyway. God knows all things and we all answer to Him, not the critics. God is the one who matters.

THE MINISTRY OWNS IT ALL

Many people have a misconception about money and ministry. Some people might be surprised to know that we do not personally own anything in this ministry—not the buildings, the equipment, the furniture, or anything else related to the VOE or OCI ministries or properties. Since we are a non-profit religious organization, we are the stewards who oversee the facility, but we do not personally own it. A 501(c)3 organization must follow rules that are different from a for-profit organization or business, and those guidelines have become more stringent over the years.

We cannot sell anything in the ministry for personal profit, nor can we use the equipment for personal gain. If someone rents the television equipment or the recording studio, the income generated must be placed back into Voice of Evangelism. The ministry also owns all of the CDs, DVDs, and books that Perry has written. All income must go back into the ministry, and a Board of Directors sets the salary and benefits for the officers of the organization. This means that they set Perry's salary, too.

Just as a denomination can remove their pastor from a church under certain circumstances, the Board of Directors could remove Perry from his position under certain circumstances. Of course, we have a great board of wonderful men who have the best interests of the ministry in mind. Each year they review detailed financial reports, including income and expenditures.

We personally own the house we live (along with the bank, since we are still making payments). We own three vehicles, not counting the one our son owns. The furniture in the house and the clothes we wear belong to us.

We do not own anything related to the ministry, and that includes ministry vehicles that the staff uses for various reasons, or even the plane or the hanger at the airport. All things connected to the ministry were purchased through resource sales, donations and offerings, and all things belong to the Kingdom of God and are used for such. We have worked hard since 1982 to ensure that anyone who gives offerings to the ministry can have complete confidence that the income is used for the work of the Kingdom.

NOBODY CAN CARE FOR YOUR BABY LIKE YOU CAN

Any business owner or CEO can acknowledge that no employee can care for your business the way you can. If you are the founder of any type of ministry or business, you attempt to hire qualified individuals who will impart their gifting to enhance the success and growth of the business or ministry. At VOE, we typically hire people we have known for many years, and who have a love for the ministry. We don't run employment ads. We want to know the people who labor among us.

To Perry and me, the Voice of Evangelism Outreach Ministry is similar to raising a newborn infant. It was birthed when he was a teenager and had to be cared for as it matured into a global ministry. When a man and woman choose to have a child, the child will begin as a thought before it is conceived as a seed and begins to form, and then is birthed. It must be protected, even in the earliest years.

Voice of Evangelism was birthed with a thought and the God-given dream of a seven-point outreach plan. A seed was planted when something of value was exchanged for five-hundred printed books. Then that money was seed to print another book, and then another and another. The books were followed by cassettes, videos, and a small magazine. Perry guarded the ministry for five years; then after marriage, I joined with him and continued to help him reach more souls.

The VOE ministry grew from two people—Perry and me—to about twenty-three full and part-time employees. We now have a team of the finest and most dedicated administrative assistants, studio editors, and other employees of any ministry. There is one thing we understand, though. No matter how dedicated the team is, nobody can carry and care for your "baby" the same way as the person who conceived and birthed the baby. Our full-time employees normally work eight hours, and most clock out and go home by five. But sometimes Perry and I are at the office, long after the staff is gone, taking care of ministry. We are both involved in the OCI ministry on Tuesday and Thursday nights while most of the employees are at home for the evening. When it is a business or ministry that *you* birthed, you will work beyond the five o'clock check out time.

A babysitter does not have the same concern for the baby she cares for as the biological mother does. She is simply doing a job that she is paid for, and she must be trusted by the parents to take responsibility and feed, protect, and care for the child as though it were her own. Nobody will care for VOE as much as we do, unless they adopt the "child" as their own. We do have some long-term staff members who care for the ministry and work above the call of duty, because they have "adopted" the ministry and treat it as though it was their own. These become the employees who are the most loyal and protective of God's vision.

As a parent, you are always concerned about your child, even when they marry and have their own children. You cannot separate yourself from your biological seed because they are your flesh and blood. You think about them in the morning and at night. You want updates and details about their lives, and you will continue to be this way until the day you die. The same is true with ministry. It is a calling. It must be protected like a parent guarding an infant. Nobody can care for the business or ministry "baby" like the parents who gave it life.

WORKING FOR THE CROWN

Our ministry partners have heard Perry joke that, when he receives his heavenly reward, he hopes to have a crown so large that someone who didn't get one will have to haul his around. What he means is that he invests money, time, and energy to advance the Kingdom of God on earth, knowing that he will enjoy eternal benefits in the life to come—which will include a crown that he can lay before Christ's feet.

We know that special crowns will be rewarded to those who faithfully served the Lord and worked in the harvest field, reaching the lost and gathering them into God's Kingdom. Jesus warned his followers that it would be possible to lose their crown (Rev. 3:11). I won't try to explain the theology of what happens when you do not obey God or work for the Kingdom, but I will tell you something that has stayed with me.

I've heard Perry preach on the rewards that will be received at the judgment seat of Christ. The twenty-four elders have crowns that they will remove from their heads and place at the feet of Jesus. These crowns are given to those who were overcomers and were faithful to Jesus when they lived on earth. If anyone makes it to heaven but loses their crown, they will never have anything to place at the feet of Jesus. Imagine having a crownless head, indicating that you failed in your obedience to God. Someone else will receive your reward on judgment day because you were too greedy or too busy to help and minister to others.

Throughout the Bible, the Lord promised His people blessings in every area of their lives — from healthy children to strong, productive animals. He promised to bless their farms and families if they obeyed His Commandments. This blessing was released upon the people because they were willing to be obedient to God's Word and His call. Obedience to God, which includes but is not limited to giving, will always bring an open window. That might include new opportunities, new connections, and open doors for increase in your life. We can expect different forms of blessing to grow out of acts of obedience, and fruit to grow from our seeds planted into ministry.

Some people invest their money in possessions instead of concentrating on their eternal reward. It is possible for any believer to receive blessings in this life and in the life to come. But some choose to receive their reward in this life rather than the life to come, because they are bound to material possessions and the building of their own personal kingdom on earth. We believe that God will bless us in this life and give us eternal rewards in the life to come, but we must be obedient in this life. If you have a choice between the two, it is much better to have an eternal reward than to receive your reward only in this life.

CHAPTER 10

MAMA P AND PAPA P

A ROUND THE AGE of fifty, Perry came to me with an announcement that probably made the angel Gabriel nervous. He said, "Hey, I want to have a couple more kids!"

"Are you kidding me?" I laughed. "Do I look like Sarah?" I reminded him that this chick has quit laying eggs, and there would be no more babies. We knew it would be a while before we had grandchildren, because Amanda is too young and marriage doesn't appear to be on the near horizon for Jonathan. We even talked about adoption.

When a person has a true desire to have children, it could be a desire imparted by the Lord for the purpose of having spiritual sons and daughters, and not necessarily flesh and blood children running through your house. Bea Ogle, the founder of our Daughters of Rachel prayer ministry, was never able to conceive children. In 1981, when the Lord inspired her to raise up a team of women to pray for Perry and the ministry, she had no idea it would grow to over 1,600 intercessors, many of whom consider her their spiritual mother. If Bea had birthed natural children, she might have had grandchildren in her house and never had the time to birth one of the most important branches on the VOE tree. So while she had no natural sons or daughters, she has many spiritual ones. She is admired and respected by all the VOE partners.

God plants specific desires in us that become seeds within our heart. A person's desire to help the poor has led people to the mission fields where they minister in poverty stricken nations. The desire to love the fatherless has motivated thousands to build or support orphanages. The desire to care for the abused has birthed inner city ministries or shelters for battered women. Human needs birth ministries that are founded and fueled by love and desire. Everything begins with a desire to make a difference.

About the same time that Perry said he wanted to have more children, he received an unexpected word from the Lord. The Holy Spirit gave him instruction and dropped within him the desire for a new assignment—to be a spiritual father to a young generation.

With so many marriages ending in divorce, with children being tossed from parent to parent, and with fathers walking out on their children, there is a void in the hearts of many young people. Many of the personal problems—rebellion, substance abuse, pre-marital sex, and so on—can stem from a root of rejection. These young people attempt to fill their emptiness with dangerous relationships, alcohol, and drugs. Both of us feel compassion toward the young people who are struggling with these bondages.

How would Perry minister to a generation of youth, when for thirty-five years he has been marked as an evangelist? Since the 1990s and because of television, most people who recognize his name associate him with prophecy preaching. That is not the only thing he preaches, but still he is viewed as a prophetic minister who also emphasizes Hebraic roots of Christianity. Also, being fifty and shifting toward a younger generation was a stretch in his mind.

When he began sharing this word and the burden God had given him, someone commented, "Well it looks like Perry is in a mid-life crisis. He's wearing jeans and wanting to hang around younger people." He reminded the person that this was not his idea. It was God's revelation for this season.

The Lord began to confirm that Perry had a word for this generation and that he would, indeed, be received by the younger generation as a voice to speak into their lives. Our friend Karen Wheaton invited us to the summer Ramp Conference, where Perry was a speaker. Karen's dynamic ministry reaches tens of thousands of young people, and during this conference over five thousand youth filled the convention center, with most sitting on the floor as close as they could get to the front. That night hundreds were baptized in the Holy Spirit. The same thing was repeated the following year at Winter Ramp. Karen then invited Perry to minister at the Ramp Conference and her School of Ministry in Hamilton, Alabama.

Perry joined with Mark Casto and his services on Tuesday night at the Extreme in Cleveland. Mark preaches three Tuesdays each month and Perry once a month. The worship, anointing, and flow of the Spirit are so strong that the attendance has grown from about twenty youth to a nice mix of children, teens, college students, young couples, and older adults, in a facility that seated 250 before moving into the new facility.

In the regional conferences, there has also been a shift in the ages of those attending. Recently we have noticed an increase in the number of teens and young couples. Parents bring their children, as young as age five, and tell us they never miss Perry's program and want him to sign a book they purchased. It may seem odd that children of that age would be interested in an in-depth teaching from the Bible. But the children are fascinated by props and the programs from Israel. We have a 23-year old and an 11-year old, so we know a few things about this generation. We also have discovered that this generation is presence-driven and not program-driven.

The traditional church has been misled into thinking that they must come up with a new angle or a new program to reach the unreached. But there is a generation that would rather be in God's presence than at the best movie or restaurant in town. They will worship for hours and sit on the floor while you preach, and then pray in the altars until the church closes. This is the generation that God promised would experience the outpouring of His Spirit.

When we purchased the OCI property, one of the first projects was to remodel the old barn and host a Thursday night prayer gathering that we now call, "Fire Night at the Barn." This barn was an old, dilapidated structure on the OCI property that was refurbished and made into a lower storage area and an upper room prayer area. The first time Perry took a dozen young people to the dilapidated building and announced,

"We're going to pray here," there was silence among them. But now the barn is used from spring to the late fall until the weather becomes too cold to meet in this unheated building. Attendance ranges from sixty to as many as one hundred thirty who meet in the upper room and pray until it echoes across the cornfield. In the colder months we have been meeting at the VOE building. We just started streaming the prayer meeting live from about eight to ten o'clock at night, as thousands join us around the world for fire night at the barn.

When the word of the Lord came to build a gathering place for this generation to create a hub for revival and a place to be trained in ministry leadership, we purchased seventy-eight acres of property that is connected by a small paved road to the VOE property. The architects began to design and the contractors were hired. From the dust arose a vision in stone and steel, the Omega Center International that houses up to 4,100 people.

When we began this project, someone posted on the internet, "Why in the world would anyone want to pray in a barn?" and somebody else mocked, "There is no such thing in the Bible as a prayer barn." Perry replied, "I think God likes barns, since Jesus was born in a stable." We also received a long letter from someone telling Perry that he shouldn't waste his time with a bunch of young people, but should stay in church where he could do the most good. Clearly this person had never read the prophecy that, in the last days, God would pour out His Spirit upon all flesh, including sons and daughters.

After the Lord gave Perry the word to father a generation, he became connected with Mark Casto. Mark was a young minister in town who worked with Dr. T. L. Lowery at the time, and Mark had organized a group of young people who met each Tuesday night at Dr. Lowery's ministry center. One night Perry showed up unexpectedly at the Extreme to speak to Mark and share the word he received about being a father to a generation. Without Perry's prior knowledge, Mark shared that he had been on a twenty-one-day fast after the Lord told him to pray for Perry's heart to turn to the younger generation.

From that moment, we looked for property to build a gathering place for this generation. This facility, called OCI (Omega Center

International) is a beautiful seventeen-million-dollar building that houses the Tuesday night services and the main event, conferences, and youth gatherings.

Once Perry made known to others the will of God for this ministry, he began to gather a group of youth leaders within the Extreme ministry and mentor them in the basics of ministry. He found a small church building in town, located just a few miles from VOE, to rent for weekly services. The Tuesday night services began to grow until the place was filled each week.

From the beginning, the youth gave us a new title that has stuck like glue. We are Papa P and Mama P, with the P representing our names. When the youth began to address us in these terms, a few of the traditional older believers thought that was disrespectful and that Perry should be addressed as Reverend or Pastor. But Perry has always preferred being called by his first name and not by a traditional title, such as reverend or evangelist.

There is also another reason why youth and spiritual leaders have a bonding like that of a parent. It is based on a Scripture in Malachi 4:5-6 and is a passage that was the theme of Pastor Mark's ministry when he started the Extreme years ago. It reads: "Behold, I will send you Elijah the prophet before the coming of the great and dreadful day of the Lord: And he shall turn the heart of the fathers to the children, and the heart of the children to their fathers, lest I come and smite the earth with a curse."

As the church enters the time known as the last days or the time of the end, God has promised that a great outpouring of His Spirit will be released among the sons and daughters (Acts 2:17). The prophet Elijah, who was translated into heaven, will return to Jerusalem in the future. But there is a spirit of Elijah which is the same power that entered John the Baptist in Luke 1:17. When John began to baptize men in the Jordan River, some thought he was the prophet Elijah. He was not Elijah, but he came in the "spirit and power of Elijah." A great multitude gathered together to listen and watch John as he rebuked hypocrites, baptized believers, and spoke of the coming Messiah.

We believe that, as the church enters the time of the end, there will no longer be a generation gap between the older and younger people. Instead, the Spirit of God will bridge all gaps until age will become insignificant and the only thing that will matter is the anointing, the outpouring, and a relationship with God.

NAMING THE OCI PROPERTY

We had just purchased the seventy-eight acres of property for the future Gathering Place and a youth camp, and we wanted a name that would match the vision. We were preaching at a church when we were introduced to a young autistic man in his twenties who did not speak, but would carry a board with the alphabet printed on it. When he wanted to say something, he would place the board on a flat surface and, taking his mother's hand, he would use her finger to touch each letter and spell out the words he wanted to say. He seldom looked at the board, but he could move his mother's hand almost as fast as a person could type on a keyboard.

He heard from the Lord and would give someone a word using this method. He would cup his hand over his ear and whistle. He told his mother years ago that, when he did this, he heard the voice of God speaking to him. Perry and I were very moved by this gift the Lord had given him. This young man gave us details about our family and children that he never would have known and only the Lord could have told him.

This is the young man who heard from the Lord about the name we were to give the youth project. Using the board he pointed out, "It is to be called the Omega Ranch Project." He was unaware that Perry had already heard the Spirit of the Lord emphasize the word Omega. Perry asked, "What should the name of the facility be?" Repeating the same pattern, the young man spelled, "Omega Center International."

That is why the name of the entire project is listed as the Omega Ranch Project, while the large gathering place is called Omega Center International. This is a name that we believe came through a human vessel who had certain physical limitations, but whose spirit and mind are connected more sensitively to the Holy Spirit than we typically see in most Christians.

We are thankful for everything the Lord has already done, and we look forward to what He still has in store for this Omega Ranch Project. We are seeing God grow the ministry as the youth marry and are having children. One week at the Bradley County Hospital were three women from OCI who were all having babies. One of the nurses commented, "I want to know what's in the water at that place!"

There are several things that Perry and I are certain of. We know that we are in the perfect will of God by moving in the direction we are headed. We know that God has great plans for the project, including a leadership academy and the youth camp. We are also convinced that the Lord has a special plan for a mighty, end-time revival for the Cleveland area.

The vision involving this OCI ministry came after a personal experience that occurred in our family several years ago. During a serious crisis, Perry told the enemy that he would pay for attacking someone we love. Today, Perry is on a mission with fire in his heart and motivation to defeat the darkness in the lives of young people and build God's kingdom through the salvation and deliverance of multitudes.

CHAPTER 11

I'M NOT GOING TO BE A FARMER'S WIFE

T HE UPPER SECTION of the OCI property, which is visible from Urbane Road, houses the gathering place and parking lot. Much of the land either was or currently is farmed. When we bought the place, I walked over the land and looked at all the corn and said, "I am not going to be a farmer's wife."

One year later I found myself on my knees in a freshly plowed field, planting seedlings in the ground for a row of tomato plants. I said, "Well, I'm not the farmer's wife. I'm the farmer." That first year, I learned many things I didn't know about planting, weeding, fertilizing, growing, and harvesting. Everything about farming is parallel to some of the spiritual truths mentioned in the Bible.

In the Bible, the seed generally references the Word of God. The ground represents the different conditions of a person's heart and their ability to receive the Word and see it produce fruit (results) in their lives. When farming, the soil must have objects removed from the ground that would keep the seed from taking root. The ground is prepared through plowing, which softens the soil before the seed is planted.

This reminds me of two groups of people in church: those whose hunger for God has prepared their hearts for the Word and they receive it with joy, while others are uninterested and paying no attention to the message. Calloused and stony hearts often have roots of bitterness; thus the seed will not grow.

The seed must also have ample rain, but not too much. Our garden is next to a creek that occasionally overflows during heavy rains. When this happens, the field becomes flooded and the topsoil and seeds can be washed away. Sudden storms in life, such as an accident, the death of a child, a potentially deadly disease and so on, can bring a flood of fear, doubt, and unbelief that washes away the faith and seeds of the Word that has been planted. We have known people who experienced an unexpected tragedy they could not explain and, instead of turning to God for strength, they turned from Him in anger. All of the messages they had heard and prayers they had prayed were suddenly thrown out the door as they accused God of being unjust.

One problem I noticed with the garden was that some weeds are unusual. A particular thorny weed, if allowed to grow, will nearly take over the garden within a week. This weed can be removed only by pulling it up by the root, because if you cut it, the thing will multiply like rabbits. We were on a ten-day trip one time and we returned to find that these ugly, thorny weeds had grown taller than the food we planted. If you don't deal with this weed right away, it will become so interwoven with the roots of your plants they you can damage the plant when you pull up the weed.

These thorn weeds can choke the growth of the other plants. In the same way, the thorns in our life can be the many cares of life that overwhelm us on a daily basis. We become so busy with family activities and work that these things choke our prayer time and intimacy with God. Soon the spiritual energy is drained from us and we are being choked from the joy of the Lord. In gardening, it takes time to deal with weeds. They have a take-over spirit, and you have to get rid of them if you expect a successful harvest.

The most important lesson was the harvest. When the time came to pick the food from the vines and plants, all of the hard work paid off. We had an abundance of squash, and the cucumbers seemed to multiply every day. Tomatoes were causing the vines to droop to the ground, and we were loaded down with cantaloupe.

The natural lesson with a spiritual parallel is that we must get rid of the weeds if we want the seeds to grow. And we cannot allow the storms to wash away the seeds or we will not have a harvest.

Connected to our ministry are several fine organizations that assist women in addiction recovery. One is a very effective organization located in Athens, Tennessee called Women at the Well. The other is called Women of Hope and is directed by Connie and David Herring.

Years ago Perry was ministering in Connersville, Indiana when he saw a group of ladies from Women of Hope giving their cardboard testimonies. The Lord spoke to him to ask Connie if she would consider moving the ministry to Cleveland. Months later VOE purchased a large house with fourteen bedrooms, seven baths, and three kitchens. We have witnessed the physical, spiritual, and emotional transformation of so many women through both of these ministries. Four babies have been born to women who entered the Hope House; and thankfully, all of them are in excellent health, which we believe is due to the mercy of God and the prayers of believers.

For the past several years, we have taken a section of the garden on the OCI property and planted vegetables that we later can in the nearby kitchen on the property. Here we teach these women how to prepare and can the food. The Women of Hope also work in the garden and help maintain it.

Gardening is definitely one of my enjoyable past times. I have always enjoyed gardening flowers, and we have numerous flowers and plants in the backyard at home. I told Perry that, if I should pass before he does, do not tell people to send money somewhere in lieu of flowers. Tell them to send flowers, because I want my corpse to be surrounded by every flower imaginable. He reminded me that I won't be seeing or smelling them, but I said that's okay; I want flowers.

If you cannot have a large garden, you might try container or straw gardening for your back yard. For several years I took bails of straw (four to six of them) that I purchased at a local farm store. Keep the bale intact and place it about fourteen inches from the side of the house, making sure it gets good sunlight. I cut a circular hole about eight to twelve inches deep on the top and placed potting soil in the hole. You can, for example, place two tomato plants in that hole. Our plants grew tall, and we had an abundance of vegetables that we ate throughout the summer.

We enjoy canning food. This has become a lost art in America, because most people eat out or buy prepackaged food. With smaller families and both parents working outside the home, people don't have the time or see the necessity to can food any longer. However, with canning, we have garden food during the winter months. We eat beans, vegetable soup, beets, chow-chow, squash and other foods that we grew and canned. This saves money, too. With rising food prices, droughts, the threat of famines, earthquakes, and other natural disasters that could destroy the food supply, it is good to have your own garden.

DISCOVERING MY MINISTRY

Over the years, sincere people have told me privately, "I believe the Lord is going to raise you up to preach!" I just smile and laugh a little. One of the first things Perry made clear before we married was that he did not need another preacher in the family, or even a singer or a piano player. He simply wanted a wife who would help him, feed him, take care of the house, and raise the children. I prefer to be behind the scenes. I will help set up meetings, meet with staff and volunteers, and put out little fires before they become big ones. Just imagine if I talked as much as Perry. He talks enough for three people!

When people think of ministry, two things come to mind. The first is standing on a platform speaking or engaging in music ministry. The second is teaching classes or doing other types of paid work in a local church. These are all ministries of the local congregation.

However, what about nursery workers, greeters, and parking attendants? What about outreach ministries, such as community service, prison ministry, nursing home ministry, bus ministry, world mission projects and more, most of which are run by volunteers? A large congregation would be helpless without the volunteers, whose work is vital to the ministry.

For me, my primary ministry was to help my husband and raise our children. But in the early days, I worked the resource table each night at revivals and duplicated the cassette messages. Working that table sounds like an easy job, and now we have an entire team of volunteers who do this. But for years, it was my job to run cassettes, type labels, sell products, answer questions, and watch Jonathan after he was born. This was my ministry and it was important for the growth of the Voice of Evangelism.

My second ministry was bookkeeper. Before there were personal computers, all record keeping was done in ledger books, which now seems ancient. Orders and donations were recorded by hand. As the official secretary of the Voice of Evangelism, I oversaw all aspects of the ministry related to paying the bills, balancing the checkbook, and keeping track of all this.

We have kept all the ledgers with the names of the "7-a-month-club" tape partners who supported the ministry with seven dollars a month; and in return, we selected a message that month and sent it to the members. In the 1982 ledger, just before we were married, are listed seventy-four names of monthly tape club partners. Among these names are ten families who still actively support the ministry. One of the original ministry partners, Mrs. Ray Gill from Rock, West Virginia, went to be with the Lord many years ago. She faithfully gave ten dollars a month until she passed away. The ministry and its outreaches were not built by a lot of large donors, but by many precious believers who sent five, seven, or ten dollars a month.

In April of 1982, the month we were married, the total income from mailed donations, tape and book sales, and the tape of the month club was $867.75 for the entire month. This is why we could not afford to hire an employee. That same monthly income for the year totaled $7,232.35.

By the early 1990s, the tape club had grown to hundreds and soon to thousands of partners. Donations were increasing and it was becoming more difficult for me to stay on the road, and then return home to do all the ministry work that needed to be done. I was overwhelmed with the amount of mail, correspondence, bills to be paid, and so on. We prayed that the Lord would help us find a bookkeeper who could take over this work for the ministry.

During one of our Pigeon Forge conferences, we were eating with friends when one of them recommended that we ask Susan Mason to come and work for us. Susan lived in Indiana and already had a job. We prayed, then asked her if she was interested. She was hired, and she and her sister and mother moved to Cleveland. She still works for the ministry and does a great job. The CPA says she maintains some of the best records in line with IRS regulations of any ministry that he has seen.

The ministry continued to grow, and we have a much larger staff today. Another job that I now have is to oversee staff meetings. Perry gets frustrated with meetings, and over the years we realized it would be best for me to be in charge of the VOE staff meetings. It has been several years since he has been directly involved in a staff meeting. That is not to say he has no opinions on the matters. But his idea of a meeting is, "tell me what you need to tell me in five minutes and let's get out of here." My idea of a meeting is to discuss the details until there is a clear resolution or plan.

After I began home schooling and started spending less time on the road, Perry took several men from the office with him when he traveled, and Larry and Gina Bean also come along to many meetings. Ron and Virginia Rowe are long-time volunteers who oversee the CD and DVD duplication team, and they were sent to us from God. With the pressure of traveling and bookkeeping off my shoulders, I could concentrate on homeschooling, caring for the house and the children, answering personal letters and emails, and so on. Our daughter Amanda and I still attend some of the larger conferences throughout the year, but with Amanda involved with OCI and the local church, that keeps me home quite a bit.

I also discovered a ministry gift that I have, although some would never classify it a ministry. In the Bible is a ministry of helps (1 Cor. 12:28). The word *helps* can also be a New Testament word for relief.

Thus the ministry of helps is designed to bring relief to other believers. This relief comes in various forms, but Paul spoke about individuals who refreshed him (2 Tim. 1:16). This refreshing was not just a visit to uplift his spirit; it also referred to provision of lodging and food.

In the mid-1980s, when we began to conduct our annual conferences in Pigeon Forge, all of the restaurants were closed by dark. We had a ministry team of fifteen to twenty-five people who needed to be fed after the service. I decided to bring cooking utensils from home and start cooking for them each night after the services. I did this in Pigeon Forge and in Dalton, Georgia. By the time we held the conference at Abba's House, we had the meals catered.

During one fall meeting in Dalton, Perry felt that I was a Martha who was allowing the cares of ministry to keep me from enjoying the ministry in the sanctuary, as I would spend that time preparing food. He gave me a sharp rebuke and said that, from now on, people would have to be responsible for their own food. He was not angry at the people, but he didn't want me to miss the meetings each night.

As he turned, the Lord sharply rebuked him and spoke to his spirit saying, "Why are you taking her ministry from her? This is her ministry to the people. I gave her the ability to cook and a gift of hospitality!" Perry repented to God and apologized to me and said, "This is your ministry. I am not going to touch it. You're the best at this of anyone I know. So keep on blessing people with your hospitality."

This is one of the reasons I oversaw the construction of a kitchen on our youth ranch property. The kitchen has been named Pam's Kitchen, and we have prepared food for special events here, in addition to canning from the garden. After its initial construction, we held cooking classes for the young ladies in the ministry who felt they did not know how to cook. Several single guys wanted to learn the art of cooking as well, so we had both gals and guys in the classes.

While I am sure Perry is biased, he has always bragged on my cooking abilities. Before we were married, when I took care of the Skelton children, I also helped prepare dinner many times for the family. So I had some early experiences in my teen years with meal preparation. When I met Perry he weighed 145 pounds. Today he weighs around 225. Apparently he enjoys my cooking because he has grown quite a bit from eating it. He tells me that I should do a cooking DVD of my favorite recipes. I probably will not do that, but I might create a cookbook one of these days.

Years ago, when small churches needed money, the ladies would cook pies or dinners in the church's kitchen and sell them to raise funds. Had it not been for these women, many churches would have suffered financially. The gift of providing a good meal was a method used to bring income for the ministry.

I have heard Perry talk about his early years growing up in Big Stone Gap, a rural community in southwestern Virginia. The ladies would spend a day in the basement of the church preparing fried chicken dinners or pies. As a kid, he might sneak over to the church and pick out a peach or apple pie. The money was raised for various projects, including paying the church bills. In the church kitchen was a flour bin which held the flour used for cooking. He talks about the time his mother opened the bin and a rat, covered in flour, jumped out.

Never think that what you do for ministry has little significance. Who are the first people you meet when you arrive at church? Typically they are the parking lot attendant and the greeter standing at the door. These may seem like unimportant jobs for unassuming people, but church surveys indicate that the friendliness and concern of these two groups of people can determine whether a person visits the church again or never returns. Nursery workers or the people involved in children's ministry can bring a child closer to God, or have the opposite effect. We are all members of the body and Christ is the head. Each part of the body has a purpose, and we must work together and present our individual gifts so that we release a corporate blessing upon the body.

THE CALLING OF MOTHERHOOD

Some people don't consider motherhood a calling. If you are a stay-at-home mom or a mother who homeschools the children, don't let anybody put you down or disrespect you because you forgo an outside career to care for your family. This is the New Testament pattern that Paul spoke of, emphasizing to Timothy the importance of godly wives and mothers. The mother's influence over her children can help them to be more mature, more stable, and less allured by the world's thinking. In the early ages, up to about age thirteen, the seed of God's Word and the teaching of personal character must be instilled in your children. If you do not take time to impart into their lives, their peers and friends at school will.

A mother must do all she can to keep the culture from determining the lifestyle of her children. This is especially true with girls, as they can easily become enamored with the latest fads, clothing, and television personalities. With our daughter, when she chooses clothes, I have a 3-B rule. This might seem crude, but this is how you must speak to your children in this culture. I tell her that it doesn't matter how good she thinks she looks in an outfit; she must never show her 3-B's— her breasts, her butt, or her belly button. If she tries on anything that shows any of these, we won't buy it. She has been taught that she is a young woman who should dress modestly.

Now that we have a youth ministry, it is evident that many mothers did not teach their daughters this lesson. If somebody is going to minister on stage, they must be dressed modestly. Young men are already ticking bombs of testosterone, and it is wrong for them to come to church and have to fight mental temptation by looking at a girl who is half-dressed, exposing her cleavage, or wearing tight or low rise pants. This might sound old fashioned, but ladies, we need to have more respect for ourselves and the men around us than to dress in this manner. We should teach this to our daughters, too. We should not be responsible for sending these guys to the altar to repent for their thoughts in church.

Years ago we were in Maryland for a revival, and several young people were sitting on the front row. Before the service, I noticed an attractive young girl sitting directly in front of the pulpit wearing a mini-skirt (if you could call it a skirt), with her legs crossed and nothing left to the imagination. I went to her and kindly asked her to sit somewhere else, as I felt her outfit was not appropriate and would be a distraction to anybody who was on the platform. She got up and went to another seat.

Another time a married woman said her husband was bound by pornography and was visiting strip clubs. She asked us to pray that he would come to the revival and listen to Perry preach. Indeed, he showed up one night with his wife. They sat about five rows back, but directly in front of them was a young girl wearing a very short dress. When everyone stood and raised their hands to worship, her hands went up and so did the dress. The wife was grieved, as she noticed her husband staring at this girl the entire time. Why should a man who is fighting temptation have to go to church and fight it again because of the way some women are dressing? This is not the case of a female not knowing how to dress properly. Believe me; every woman knows exactly what she is doing and what her intentions are when she chooses her clothing.

Mothers, part of our ministry is to teach modesty to children, especially our daughters, at an early age. We could save some of our young people from falling into the trap of pre-marital sex if we would teach them from an early age that they are not subject to a liberal culture, but are men and woman of God in training.

WHEN YOU ARE TOLD YOU HAVE CANCER

It is a dreaded statement to hear that you have cancer. The "c" word brings paralyzing fear and releases a barrage of images, such as chemotherapy, loss of hair, and even death. Through our years of traveling and ministering, hundreds of times we have heard prayer requests for someone who was diagnosed with cancer. We have witnessed several of our friends and ministry partners pass away in their forties and fifties from this dreaded disease. At the same time, many have been treated and others miraculously cured through the prayer of faith.

At the Voice of Evangelism offices, two of our ladies on staff dealt with breast cancer. Thankfully, both recovered and are doing well. I have heard the prayer requests and felt compassion, but when the words, "You have cancer" are spoken over you, the same emotions all others experience are instantly released in your own mind.

I have been in good health from the time Perry and I were married. There have been times of stress in the ministry, just as in any job where people work long hours under pressure. It was not always easy to eat well on the road, where your choice of restaurants might be fast food. I do have a weakness for chocolate and a sweet tooth for desserts. But I always had a yearly check-up to maintain my health and ensure there were no physical complications or disease in my body.

In 2008, during a routine mammogram, the doctor said that there was a place that needed to be watched. Another mammogram was scheduled in six months. It was difficult to wait without knowing the full situation and the outcome of the future report. The follow-up showed that I needed a biopsy. I had very early stages of cancer that was contained in a small area.

Being raised in a church that believed healing was provided in the atoning work of Christ, and having seen and heard of miracles through prayer, I was like many other women who had received the same report. As a Spirit-filled believer, if I chose surgery, was I demonstrating to God that I did not believe He was able to heal me? Was I showing a lack of faith? Would the Lord be better glorified for me to ignore the doctor's advice and begin a regimen of prayer and quoting Scriptures?

This was the first mental and emotional struggle over healing that I had experienced in my life. It is easy to believe and agree with others, but there are mental blocks and questions that arise when the circumstances are present in your own life.

At that time Perry's dad, Fred, was still living and had a strong ministry of praying for the sick. From the mid-1990s until the mid-2000s, Fred had personally seen people healed of cancer through his prayers. I knew that I also could receive healing. Perry had written a wonderful book based upon a teaching he heard from Dr. John Miller, on the power of receiving communion, as communion represents the atoning power of the blood and the body of Christ. The teaching emphasizes that, if a Christian is sick, it is possible to receive a miracle of healing through daily communion, prayer, and the Word of God.

Over the years we had received wonderful testimonies of God's healing power through the Lord's Supper. I also knew that, in Perry's own ministry, through the prayer of faith the Lord had healed people of various diseases, including cancer.

I was now at a crossroads. Should I forgo surgery and stand only on the scripture's promises, or should I proceed with surgery? I almost felt that if I had the surgery, I would be showing God that I was not trusting in Him. If you have been in this predicament, you will understand the mental struggle.

Perry gave me a significant word of wisdom when I told him my struggle. He said, "Pam, here is the key to the answer. Do you have an absolute rhema word from the Lord, a quickened word, that you will be healed if you do not have surgery? If can say that you have no doubt and your spirit is quickened with faith, then don't have surgery. But if there is any bit of doubt that would make you lie awake at night and wonder if everything is okay, then have the surgery."

I told him that I knew God could heal me. However, I did not have that quickened rhema word that brings absolute faith in a situation. At times I would lie in bed and wonder what *could* happen down the road if I avoided surgery. He said, "Then have the surgery and believe God that it will never come back. There is still nothing wrong with praying for healing and taking communion daily, to build your faith and show God that you trust Him for a good outcome."

That advice brought peace to my spirit, and I told the doctor I would opt for surgery. At the same time, I began to ask God for complete wholeness in my body, also praying and believing that the cancer had not spread. Taking daily communion helped renew my mind and maintain confidence in God's promises. I had the surgery, and tests indicated that I was now free from cancer in my body. I maintain a yearly check-up to confirm that all is well.

This experience taught me several things. First, a bad report does not indicate defeat. Our first reaction to negative news is always, "Wow! How did this happen to me?" That is followed by a barrage of negative images and thoughts, including the possibility of death. A negative report is not a final indicator that things are going to end up badly.

The second lesson was that I cannot base my healing on how someone else might have been healed. In the Bible, Jesus healed several blind people, and all were healed by a different method. The miracle might be the same, but the method can be different. If I hear that someone was impressed to eat a certain diet for six months and they received healing, this does not mean that the same action will work for everybody.

Someone else is prayed for and receives instant healing, but others have hands laid upon them according to James 5:14 and see no manifestation of healing. They must continue to believe for an answer by faith.

And lastly, choosing surgery should not be considered a sign of weakness. I was the same dedicated Christian before surgery as after. Doctors were not given to us for evil, but for good. The goal of a doctor should be to assist a person in recovering their health, living longer, and defeating sickness and disease. Each believer must perceive their faith level and pay attention to the direction the Lord is leading them when they receive a negative report.

With three women on our staff who have dealt with breast cancer, I will say that one of the most important steps for prevention is regular checkups to catch cancer in the earliest stages. I want us all to live long and blessed lives.

WHEN HEALING DOES NOT COME

How do we explain the situations when prayers of faith are prayed and people stand in agreement for healing, yet the healing does not occur? The common explanation is that faith was weak or there was too much unbelief. One time I heard a minister say that some people have so much faith that, when something bad happens, they have no theology to accommodate a tragedy.

Sometimes people who believe God heals will change their theology to accommodate death. But we do not always know why someone passes away after we have prayed, and we must not alter our belief in the promises of God based upon lack of results.

Before Perry and I were married, there was a wonderful, godly woman in our church whom we called Mama Booth. This woman of great faith was diagnosed with pancreatic cancer and was experiencing constant pain and suffering. The church prayed often on her behalf, believing God for her healing. I called Perry while he was on the road and asked him to pray, but several days later I had to call to tell him Mama Booth had passed away.

The church members were disturbed, because much prayer had been offered for her recovery. Perry prayed about this situation, and the Holy Spirit revealed that she wanted to go to be with the Lord. When a person wills or chooses to go to heaven, no prayers can hold them on earth.

After the funeral, the pastor's wife informed us that Sister Booth told her that her work was finished and she wanted to be with the Lord. She knew that the church was praying and appreciated their prayers, but it was her desire to leave her suffering body and be with Christ. This was a comfort to the church, as they realized it wasn't that God didn't hear their prayers; it was that God honored her will and choice to be with Him.

Perry's dad, Fred, was a man of great faith and deep prayer. If you had a sudden emergency and needed one person to call for prayer, you would call him. Sometimes it seemed that he had a direct, private line to heaven that most people did not have. Through over sixty years of ministry, hundreds of people were healed of every imaginable type of disease or affliction. These results were manifested through the Holy Spirit gifts of faith and healing.

When Fred was forty-nine, he learned that he was dealing with the early stages of diabetes. It progressed, and with his travel schedule and desire to fast, he did not keep a proper routine for eating, and he often ate things a diabetic should not eat. By the time he was in his seventies, the diabetes had taken its toll on his eyes, heart, and kidneys.

Some people could not understand how a man could pray such effective prayers of faith and see miracles of healings, but not receive his own healing. One time he and Perry discussed the issue, and Perry reminded his dad that that our physical body wears out over time. He also noted that Elisha received a double portion of the spirit of Elijah; however, Elisha died of a sickness. After his death, Elisha's bones could raise a dead soldier! It is a mystery how the power in his bones would bring a man back from the dead, but this same power did not heal the prophet when he became sick (2 Kings 13:14-20).

Fred never defeated diabetes and passed away in 2011. His organs eventually shut down, and for several days before he died, he was not able to eat or drink. But his sickness did not negate sixty years of ministry and countless answered prayers and healings. Many times we will pay little attention to the high blood pressure, diabetes, high cholesterol and other warning signs, until we have some form of damage to our body. It should be our intent to care for our body, soul, and spirit and live a life of wholeness, so that we can fulfill all of our days and complete every assignment.

Eventually, we all will die or be changed in the twinkling of an eye at the return of Christ. We must believe that it is God's will for us to have a long life, and that we will live out all of our assigned days. Then, when our time arrives, we will joyfully pass from the temporal to the eternal world, joining those who have preceded us. It is not a tragedy to leave this earth and be with Jesus, and we know that the separation is just temporary. We will see them again if we live for Christ.

CHAPTER 12

THE PERRY YOU
MIGHT NOT KNOW

T HE LORD ENTRUSTED Perry at a very young age with the vision of the Voice of Evangelism ministry. As one minister said, "At that time, Perry was the voice of nothing, yet he believed he would have a voice to the nation." He also developed a seven-point outreach plan after much fasting and prayer, and that became the foundation for all ministry outreaches.

He realized early in ministry that, if he only reached the people sitting under his ministry, he would be limited in the number of people he would reach in his lifetime. One way to expand his voice was through media, printed material, and taped messages. His first booklet was *Precious Promises for Believers*, and he paid for the printing of five hundred copies of the book by trading in his set of drums that he played in his father's church. This was a seed that has produced the fruit of around eighty printed titles that Perry has written over the years.

He sometimes tells his personal testimony of how he battled mental oppression and even depression at the beginning of his ministry. This lasted about five years, until we were married. That is when it broke. Being such a reclusive person, only a few close friends knew he was dealing with it. He stayed in his room studying and praying all day, and came out to eat or go to church. He kept the blinds in the room closed, and he did not like being out in the sun. His sleep patterns were odd, as he might stay up all night, or for as long as twenty-four hours.

Most might assume this was just the life of a single young man. But something was happening that he didn't know how to battle. He would go into deep despair, then work his way out of it and be okay for a short time.

One of his friends who served as best man in our wedding occasionally traveled and team preached with Perry. It was Perry who introduced him to his future wife. Perry would often write and begin the letter with, "I'm depressed." It became so common that is was almost like a joke, yet he was serious. Part of this stemmed from a six-month demonic attack in which the adversary used spiritual powers to attack his mind. I won't go into that here, because Perry has written about this in other books, including one he just expanded and reprinted, called *Dealing with Hindering Spirits*.

When it came to preaching revivals, once Perry became acquainted with a pastor and the church, he would return there each year, seldom adding new churches to his itinerary. Even with invitations from dozens of new churches, he chose to continue in his familiar circuit. Meeting new people, going to a new church, and staying in the homes of pastors he did not know was challenging for him and would cause anxiety and an overwhelming sense of dread of the unknown.

Over our years of marriage, I noticed a pattern developing. When we were invited for a meal at the home of someone we didn't know, he would dread going. After eating, he was always in a hurry to leave. On the occasions when we flew to a revival, if his ticket had him sitting next to a stranger, he would change seats with me. He could not handle the pressure of speaking to someone he did not know. This made him extremely nervous, and there was no explanation for it. Once he made Jonathan sit beside a stranger on the plane. The man was rather large and Jonathan was becoming agitated as the fellow was moving into his space. Jonathan was about five at the time, and he suddenly blurted out, "Dad, why did you sit me beside this big man?" The things that come from the mouth of babes!

Over the years people have noticed that, when they personally speak to Perry, he might give a short answer and will not often engage in a long or detailed conversation. The three topics he most enjoys discussing are religion, politics, and football. Outside of that, he does not have much to say to people he does not know. He has been accused of being unfriendly or of not wanting to talk to people. But this is not the case. It would take us thirty-three years of marriage to discover one of the reasons why he is this way.

He and I were with a counselor taking a written exam to determine if there was a spectrum of autism in our family. The exam revealed that there was indeed a form of autism, called Asperger's. Perry repetitive and habitual behavior and his inability to communicate one-on-one, as well as other symptoms revealed that he has Asperger's. We discovered, however, that such individuals may have difficulty explaining their feeling to others, but they are masters at writing them down. They can be very successful and display high intelligence in the one area that they truly enjoy. They master that one area, which is usually connected with a particular subject or technology. In Perry's case, he masters the Bible.

For someone with Asperger's, there is comfort in routine, and to break any normal routine is confusing and frustrating. This explains how Perry can be alone by himself for hours at a time, without any communication from others, and be very content. When someone interrupts his routine of study at the office, he can become agitated. Because of the location of his office, he sees very few people throughout the day. He has no problem sitting at his desk for hours, readying, studying, writing, and working uninterrupted. He is learning to handle the emotional side of this issue, and the staff has come to understand his quirks and unusual manner of thinking.

There might be thousands of people in America who have this form of autism and have never been diagnosed. Large crowds of unfamiliar people make them nervous and withdrawn. Based on their personality traits, researchers speculate that some of the well-known people who might have had Asperger's included Henry Ford, Isaac Newton, Mark

Twain, Nicola Tesla, Thomas Jefferson, and even George Washington. Many computer technology experts are believed to have it.

Another challenge is the inability to read the expressions of people. If someone looks his way with a certain expression, he may assume they are thinking something that might not have even crossed the person's mind. These people also need to have one very close friend. Some people love to have many friends. Our daughter Amanda is a social butterfly, and she is most fulfilled when she is surrounded with her friends. Perry could take a dog to work and have the same friend all the time for the next five years.

If a friend is no longer part of his life, they become out of sight and out of mind. He might never speak about that person again, once they are out of sight. This is simply the way his brain works. He is consumed in the present, and past relationships that are not currently active are not on his mind.

This brings up a mystery. How can an introvert and a loner stand before thousands and boldly preach and pray for thousands? The answer is the *call* of God and the *anointing* of the Holy Spirit. Through the calling of God, the Lord gave Perry the confidence to trust that He would lead him in the proper paths and open doors for ministry. The anointing provides a boldness to minister that could not come through the power of his flesh or intellect. The way his mind is wired, he can study for hours and days on end. This explains how Perry can spend all day in one spot and be happy.

While this could be seen as a hindrance, we view it as a spiritual benefit that enables Perry to do in-depth research, and it allows him to look at that research in a different way. It might seem odd to say this, but God uses the condition for His purposes.

Once Perry began to share about the Asperger's in his meetings, we have been surprised to see the number of parents whose children also have a form of autism. It gives them hope, knowing that God can use a person's weaknesses. Perry's weakness in social interaction and one-on-one communication is overcome when he preaches by the presence of the Lord that abides in his life.

There is another side to his personality, though, which I believe comes through the Italian side of the family. Many people with Asperger's do not like to be touched or hugged. This makes them uncomfortable and can cause them to seem aloof and disconnected. The opposite is true with my husband.

He is a very affectionate person. Every day he will say to me and the kids, "Have I told you today that I love you?" He enjoys hugging us and telling us how much he loves us. In an attempt to explain his affectionate nature to the staff one time, he joked that when he was born, he could not keep milk down and the doctor was concerned about him. They kept him in the hospital for an extra two weeks, and his mother was not permitted to hold him. She could only stand at the window and look at him. He said in a serious tone of voice, "The reason I hug is because my mother didn't hold me for two weeks and it permanently damaged me."

It has helped us to understand this autism and learn what Perry must do to discipline his thinking and step out of his comfort zone to function in areas where he is weak. The reason he decided to make this public is because many Christians have a child who is dealing with similar issues. They need to know that they are not weird, but that they have a personality that allows the unique gifts that are within them to be used to benefit the lives of other people. God will use their weakness to allow them to accomplish something that a person without that weakness could not accomplish.

This should encourage anyone who has some kind of weakness that they feel makes them different from others. Be aware that God does not choose a perfect vessel, but a willing and obedient one. We know our own weaknesses, and sometimes we believe that God cannot or will not use a person with imperfections to complete a major assignment. However, the Bible is filled with examples of men and their children who would be classified today as dysfunctional. I believe God put their victories and failures in the Scripture to show us that He can use anyone with any weakness, as long as they are willing to trust Him completely. Three verses should comfort anyone who feels they have such a weakness:

"But God has chosen the foolish things of the world to put to shame the wise, and God has chosen the weak things of the world to put to shame the things which are mighty."   *- 1 Cor. 1:27 (NKJV)*

"And He said to me, "My grace is sufficient for you, for My strength is made perfect in weakness. Therefore most gladly I will rather boast in my infirmities, that the power of Christ may rest upon me."   *- 2 Cor. 12:9 (NKJV)*

"Therefore I take pleasure in infirmities, in reproaches, in needs, in persecutions, in distresses, for Christ's sake. For when I am weak, then I am strong."   *- 2 Cor. 12:10 (NKJV)*

Paul understood that we cannot operate in our own strength, but through Christ alone. God chooses obedient vessels; not perfect ones.

GROWING OLD TOGETHER

Eventually it will happen. When you are in your twenties, you never see it coming. It seems a long way off because you have your entire life in front of you. Great plans are swirling in your head like toys dancing in the imagination of a child before Christmas.

The realization begins to strike on specific birthdays—the first being the thirtieth. At thirty you think about how you coasted through your teen years and rode through your twenties. Now you're suddenly speeding into your thirties. Before you know it, here comes forty. You feel a little older, more mature, and more settled. You know where you have been and think you know where you are going. When you hit fifty you don't look back; you looked forward and realize that you can retire in fifteen years.

By the time men hit fifty, they notice white sidewalls and missing hair. They flex their muscles and wonder what happened to them. They look in the mirror and see a stomach that looks like a spare tire encircling their mid-section.

For a woman, the mirror can become her worst enemy. She wonders what happened to that young woman she had been looking at all those years. There's more gray hair, another wrinkle, another line telling her that time is catching up with eternity. Her favorite dress no longer fits, and she's pretty sure it's not the dry cleaner's fault. She is sure she needs a new bathroom scale, because this old one is off by at least twenty pounds.

When her children bring over their children, she is reminded that she is getting older. Mother has now become Grandmother. All around us are signs that we are mortal beings who have a set amount of time left to complete our assignments.

Several years before Perry's dad passed away at age 78, they were together in the house when Fred began to notice that there was a good bit of gray in Perry's hair. Fred reached over and touched Perry's hair and said, "Son I hate to see that. I hate to see you getting older." By this time the diabetes was taking a toll in Fred's body. He was losing his vision, and soon his kidneys would begin to fail and he would be on dialysis.

The words of his father began to affect Perry when he crossed the age fifty threshold. Perry might be over fifty in earth time, but like many people, he is still a boy trapped in a man's body. Our bodies age, but our spirits don't.

Perry still enjoys playing pranks on people, which he learned from his Granddad Bava. John Bava lived into his early 80s, and until the last few months of his life, he seemed to be much younger. He got up early every morning and always kept himself busy with work. He always laughed and told jokes. He could make anybody laugh. Every day Granddad traveled off the mountain from Davis, West Virginia to Elkins so he and Lucy could eat at the Western Steer Steak House. After he died, the restaurant hung a picture of him on the wall, calling him their most-valued customer.

One time Granddad was at Wal-Mart talking to a group of men in their sixties and seventies. He was nearly eighty years old himself. When we got into the car, he looked a little disgusted. We said, "What's going on?" He replied, "I get tired of these old men always talking about their aches and pains." Obviously he did not consider himself an old man. He would say, "You're only as old as you feel."

There is a precious woman of God named Beverly who attends our weekly youth service. At the time of this writing she is eighty-four years young and is loved by the youth and the older crowd alike. She has beautiful skin and almost no crow's feet or wrinkles. When asked her secret, she replied that she uses olive oil on her skin every day. She is proof that it works. Then there is Perry's mother, who was Perry's first secretary when he lived and worked out of his parent's home in Salem, Virginia. Now well into her 70s, she continues to work and maintains a sharp mind, as did her mother Lucy, who passed away at age 86. Working and keeping the mind active are keys to maintaining youth.

I do believe, though, that age is not a number; it is more of an attitude. Some turn forty but already act like they're sixty. Some turn sixty and could pass for forty.

Most people who are close to Perry know that he has gray hair. Usually he keeps it covered because of something Amanda said to him a few years ago. She overheard Fred and Perry talk about going down into the grave with gray hair. She began to equate gray hair with dying, so she came to her dad and said, "Daddy, you're looking older and I don't want you to have gray hair." Perry said, "I can fix that." He showed up one day with dark hair and usually maintains it to this day. Some of our older friends (including Perry's mom) tell him to leave his gray alone; the Bible says it's a crown of glory. Perry replies that he will get his crown in heaven one day; so for now, he will avoid that form of glory on earth.

We have discovered a key that helps you feel younger: hang around young people. Look at our friend Beverly. What are most widows doing at age 84? Most are hanging around people their own age. Not Beverly. She says, "I don't like hanging around those old people. All they do is complain, talk about some new medicine, or tell you how bad their kids and grandchildren are." She prefers to be around the youth and watch them worship. She spends time praying for them and giving them advice.

In the small building, our sound system was loud. Instead of complaining, Beverly would enjoy the music in another room, watching it on a flat screen television, and then come in the main sanctuary for the preaching and altar services. She became like a grandmother to so many young people who love to listen to her advice and hear her tell stories from her past. But she does not live in the past. She is a visionary who speaks about plans for the future—plans to assist young people, especially those bound by drugs and alcohol.

There is a misconception that younger people want nothing to do with elderly people, and that elderly people are out-of-touch with this generation. But Beverly is proof that is not the case. These young people sit with her and listen to her practical advice and wisdom on spiritual matters and personal discipline. She loves them, and at the same time, talks to them bluntly and openly. They love her and respect her opinions.

One of the most powerful illustrations Beverly gives was written in Perry's upcoming book, *The Judas Goat*. Here is what she said:

> *"My mother was a beautiful, yet verbally and physically abusive woman. I felt that I could never please her and was always reminded of all the times I failed and didn't meet her standard. I grew up and married. As I matured, I had difficulty and sought advice from a counselor.*
>
> *"After hearing of my mother's lack of love and how it affected me, the counselor said, 'Would you accept all of the money I have today to give you?' I replied that I would. He pulled out his wallet and there was no money in it. He searched and found two cents in his pocket and handed them to her. He asked, 'Are you mad at me?' I said, 'Of course not!' He asked why not and I replied, 'Because that was all the money you had and you gave me all you could give me.'*
>
> *"There he made the point. 'Your mother gave you all the love that she knew how to give. She only had two cents worth and no more. Don't be mad when that was all she had and all she knew how to give.' That illustration brought me freedom."*

Perry's mother, Juanita, is seventy-seven years of age and drives to work where she opens mail and inputs data on the computer. She feels that as long as she can work, it will help her mentally and physically to live a fuller life. People eventually retire from their jobs, but retirement does not mean that you cease from all activity. Take Ron and Virginia Roe. This precious couple is retired; however, they travel to Perry's conferences, duplicating the CDs and DVDs, and making them available to the attendees. They are often accompanied by other precious people who have retired, including another couple who have moved to Cleveland—Gary and Vickie Fugitt. These people are priceless to the ministry. They might be busier now than they were when they were employed in regular jobs. But they love volunteering with the VOE and OCI ministries, and they will do any form of work and activity that keeps them physically and mentally active. They are helping themselves and being a tremendous blessing to the ministry at the same time.

Perry and I have both chosen to run this leg of our race at full speed ahead, not looking back. We want as many people as possible to run with us in this race. We will run with the orphans and the fatherless, the widows and the needy, the rich and the poor, the young and the elderly, and people of every race. We will run until we cross the finish line together. When running a race and passing a baton, the fastest runners are reserved for the final leg of the race. Perry and I began this race as two young people in love, and we are going to keep working together to finish this race to the very end.

CHAPTER 13

QUESTIONS YOU HAVE ASKED

Question: During that long revival, Perry said the Lord spoke to him twice that he would marry you. Did anything similar happen to you?

Answer: No, not really. I was not aware of his interest in me until the third week of the revival. At that point, when the young people would go out to eat, he would sit beside me. Into the fourth week, he would occasionally hold my hand under the table. I remember him saying something and I thought, "That's an interesting statement; maybe he's sending me a message." The youth had eaten at Taco Casa and Perry had left his car at the church. He needed a ride back, which was about a two to three mile drive. He asked if I could drive him and I agreed. It was raining hard and the wipers were on high as they cleared the windshield. Suddenly he said, "I love to hear the rain like that. On a night like this I wish I was married." I smiled and kept my eyes on the road.

After the four-week revival he immediately traveled to Virginia Beach for his next meeting. I knew I had developed true feelings for him and, when he was gone, I missed him greatly. My sisters and close friends were concerned that Perry would go his way, find somebody else, and I would be disappointed and hurt. Yet, with all of the voices around me, something deep within me told me that he really loved me and that I really loved him.

About a month after Perry's revival, our church conducted another revival with Marcus Lamb. I didn't realize that Perry had already told Marcus that he was interested in me, and there had been a discussion between them about his break-up with the girl he had been engaged to and his interest in me.

When Marcus arrived, he asked about the young lady that Perry told him about named Pam Taylor. When he found out who I was, he was kind and friendly, but after a brief conversation he said he wanted to warn me not to get my hopes up because Perry probably has a girl he likes in every church where he preaches. Later I would learn that Perry and Marcus were close friends, and I'm sure Marcus was being ornery. We still tease him about it.

About two months later Perry told me he loved me. I knew we would get married. He has said, "If I could do one thing over again, I would have married you much earlier and gotten it over with." His second regret is that we didn't have children sooner so that maybe we would have had more.

Question: I have heard Perry say that he was engaged before he met you. Were you in love with someone else before you fell in love with him? Were you dating someone?

Answer: As with any single, teenaged girl in a large youth group, there were times when I went out to eat with one of the young men from the church, or we would go to sports events at the high school or ride together to a revival. There was never a relationship with any of them, but more a close friendship. The church was strict and they kept a close watch on the youth, which is not a bad thing.

During Perry's four-week revival at our church, one young man who was interested in me asked to talk to Perry privately one night. He was seeking advice on how to get my attention. He and Perry talked for over an hour one night. A week later, I was the person the Lord told Perry he would marry.

I'm not sure if he used his own advice when he got my attention, but he hooked me. A few days before we married, this young man called me and asked me if I knew I was doing the right thing. I told him I was. At the same time, Perry received a long letter from one of the girls he had once dated, telling him that she still thought about him. But there was nobody who could cause us to question our love or pull us away from our commitment to be husband and wife.

Question: I am sure you have heard your husband preach thousands of times, and during that time repeat certain stories and illustrations. Do you ever get tired of hearing the same message or the same stories or illustrations?

Answer: To answer this, I'll compare this to Perry going to Israel and seeing the same holy sites over and over for the past thirty years, but never getting tired of it. He says it never gets old because there are always new people who have never been there and are excited to see the places and hear the stories.

When Perry preaches the same message, it always comes out different each time, because he doesn't follow a set outline or script. It is true that he repeats stories, and people who have listened to him for years might get tired of hearing them. I can't say that I get tired of hearing them, because they reveal the power and goodness of God. And when a message is anointed of the Holy Spirit, the anointing brings life to the words being spoken. As long as Perry walks with God and maintains the anointing, he will always be my favorite preacher.

Now our children are different. Once Jonathan hears something, he never wants to hear it repeated again. This was a challenge in school, because to hear something taught more than once provokes him. He thinks he has heard all of his dad's stories, and he doesn't want to hear them more than once. Amanda enjoys her dad's preaching, but she mostly enjoys the stories because she doesn't always understand what he preaches.

Question: What was the most difficult part about having a traveling, evangelistic ministry?

Answer: Christians sometimes believe there is glamour or thrill in traveling the nation and ministering. Even young people assume this is the case. When our son Jonathan was an infant, we carried him with us on the road from the age of one month to eleven years. In each church, he made a few friends that he would see each year when we returned. Many time his friends would say, "Jonathan, you are lucky. You get to travel and stay in hotels." Jonathan would say, "No, you are, because you get to go home and sleep in your own bed."

The most difficult part of traveling as an evangelist is the traveling itself. First, we sometimes stayed in the home of a stranger and had to get to know them, eat with them, and get adjusted to following their patterns. This is why we enjoyed returning to a church where we were already acquainted with the pastor and the people.

The second difficulty was that, in the earlier years of ministry, we did not have office help. We would return home and have piles of letters, orders, and bills to work on before we left again. We had to work long hours to get caught up.

Third, once we had Jonathan and took him on the road with us, the length of the trips was harder to handle. We drove everywhere we went, whether it was to Florida, Texas or Maine. It might have taken fifteen hours one way. This is why that today, Jonathan has no interest in traveling. He says, "I got tired of it as a kid and I want to stay home."

We ate in people's homes or in restaurants most of the time, and finally we were home in December because that was the month that Perry tried not to schedule revivals. Jonathan was about two years old when he realized that I could cook a meal at home. He was so excited. From then on, he would always want me to cook when we were home. He still loves his mom's cooking.

Question: Was there ever a time when you could not pay your bills, or had a difficult time financially? I have heard stories of men who quit the ministry because the finances weren't there to continue.

Answer: When I married Perry he was already established in the ministry and had a cassette and book outreach in motion. When his parents moved from Virginia to Florida, I took care of his ministry mail at the Skelton's, where I lived at that time. Perry sent me a letter with a check for book sales from one service in New York. It was for $75. So we weren't talking about big bucks.

When we were married, we were invited to conduct a tent revival in Maine. Altogether, it took three weeks out of our schedule, including driving time. The total offering was $500, which barely covered gas, meals, and the hotel. When we returned home Perry was discouraged. He was talking about borrowing money from the bank to meet our obligations that month. We prayed about it, and the following week we went to a revival in North Carolina that extended from one week to three. The offerings covered our needs and we didn't have to borrow money from the bank.

It was always disheartening to minister for many weeks in a church, only to discover that the pastor and the church counsel had withheld half or more of the offerings the people had given the ministry. One minister took up an offering each night during a four-week revival for their evangelism fund. We learned this was his fund for his own radio program. So after preaching thirty-two services, we receive partial offerings and paid for the pastor to be on the radio. One pastor said, "The offering tonight is going toward the evangelist." But half of it never made it to the evangelist.

We traveled and had financial needs, too, and many times we walked a financial tightrope. But we give God all the glory for being our provider during these many years of ministry. On those occasions when we were short of funds, the Lord made up for the shortage. And throughout the years, the Lord enabled us to pay our debts and still expand the ministry.

Question: Looking back over your ministry, is there anything you would do differently?

Answer: I believe Perry and I have both obeyed the Lord in our personal lives and ministry. But there is one area that I would change if I could. In the first eighteen years that we were married, we hardly ever took a break. We would travel to a revival, stay two weeks or longer, return home, care for things that needed to be done with the ministry or at home, clean our clothes, repack, and head to another revival and start the process all over again. One year Perry preached 320 times.

It was years before we ever took a real vacation. Perry still feels guilty that we married on a Friday and drove the next day to a revival without taking a honeymoon. He has apologized many times for that. When he was home, he would sometimes stay at the office until after midnight getting caught up, working with Charlie and Phillip. One time I called him at ten o'clock and said, "It is a shame I have to put on this new nightgown and go to bed by myself." He said, "I'm coming home right now." And he did.

So, if I could change something, I would make him take more vacations and family time, just to get away from everything. One of my "love languages" is family time, and he has learned that we will have two vacations a year. He finally enjoys vacations and no longer sees them as a disruption of his study time.

Question: How do you homeschool, and do you believe a parent should do this if they possibly can?

Answer: I have homeschooled both of my children—Jonathan until he was eleven, and Amanda is still being homeschooled. I use a DVD program from A Beka out of Pensacola, Florida. The DVD is of a school classroom with a teacher who interacts with the students at home. They provide the books and tests, and I oversee the process for several hours a day. In our town, the homeschoolers get together for organized field trips, special events, and other activities.

Homeschooling can be time-consuming, but very fruitful. When Jonathan entered private school, he was tested and they advanced him a year because of his knowledge on all subjects. In our OCI youth group are many children who are homeschooled. I have noticed they are all intelligent, mature, balanced, and spiritually involved in the ministry. While many girls in public schools are boy crazy by age ten, these girls have a different focus. Critics say homeschoolers are not balanced and are weak in social skills. I disagree.

If you choose to homeschool, check the specific laws of your state and follow them. In the early days of our nation, much of the education and instruction came from home and from both parents. A parent must be dedicated to the cause, focused, and patient. It will take up to five hours a day and longer as the lessons becomes more difficult. If you are impatient and can't spend the time, I suggest that you keep them in a good private or public school.

Today with both parents working, we often hand our children over to a secular system for instruction. In Cleveland, we have many friends who are public school teachers, and we have very good public schools. However, for Amanda to travel with us to some of the conferences during the year, homeschooling is our best option.

Question: I had several miscarriages which were emotionally difficult for me. I was surprised to learn that you also had a miscarriage, because I would think that God's favor would be upon you to keep such a thing from happening. How did you deal with it?

Answer: First of all, I don't believe that a woman who miscarries has necessarily done anything wrong to cause the miscarriage. The favor of God is upon every believer who is walking in covenant with God; yet at times, bad things happen to God's people. There is not always an explanation for why these things happen.

In my situation, I became pregnant at age thirty-nine. At the end of about seven weeks, the doctor said, "We cannot hear the heartbeat." The decision was made to allow a few more weeks and then listen for the heartbeat. I immediately started praying for the child, even pleading with the Lord to revive the child I was carrying. One day I heard something in my spirit that startled me. The Lord spoke to me and said, "Do you want this baby to live, no matter what condition it is in?" Not knowing the condition of which the Lord was speaking, I felt a release in my spirit and began to say, "Lord, you know the future and what is best. Let your will be done in this situation."

The following week was our largest meeting of the year, the Main Event at the Grand Hotel in Pigeon Forge, Tennessee. It is always a busy week of preparation for the ministry team. It was a Monday night, and our prayer team gathered in the convention center where they always pray before Tuesday's opening night service. Our long-time friends were excited about the pregnancy and wondered if this would be the little girl that Perry saw in a vision in 1989.

But that very night, I miscarried. It was an emotionally stressful time. Perry and I wanted another child, and the miscarriage made me think I was getting too old to have another baby. Through an unusual visitation, we knew we were supposed to have another child. I became pregnant again, but in the seventh month there were complications and I was put on bed rest. Thankfully, our daughter Amanda was born on August 2, 2000. She was healthy and has been a joy to our lives.

A miscarriage can be traumatic, especially for the mother. If you become pregnant, then pray that the Lord will bless the fruit of your womb and give you a healthy child. Most women who have had miscarriages can become pregnant again. The child we miscarried will be there for us when we get to heaven, and yours will be there for you, too.

Question: Have you ever sensed that a woman was after your husband? And if so, what did you do about it?

Answer: Throughout our marriage, Perry has always tried to be cautious when dealing with women. When he travels to preach, he always takes a ministry team with him. Other male staff or team members stay where he stays, and he has security measures that he does not discuss. This is precautionary, so that no false accusations can be made against him. He has very few close female friends, all of whom are strong spiritual women of God, and the relationship is ministry-related. We both are close friends with these ladies and have been for many years. With the youth, he views them as daughters and sons.

During our entire marriage, I can only think of three occasions in which I was wary of a particular woman. I was warned about one of them in a spiritual dream. We learned that two of these women were having problems in their marriages and both later had moral failures that impacted their lives and families. One of the women seemed to want attention from Perry because she was enamored with the ministry and anointing. When I have those gut feelings, Perry pays attention.

After many years of marriage, he has acknowledged that I (as all wives do) have an intuition when it comes to women. That is because no woman knows another woman like a woman. Men are more naïve. Most of the time, they seem clueless about a woman's wrong intent.

Men should pay attention to their wife's warnings and observations when it comes to other women. Don't just think her concern is jealousy. God might be trying to protect you from a seductive woman who could strike like a serpent and ruin your life and family.

Question: What part of the ministry do you enjoy most?

Answer: I most enjoy seeing the Lord change lives. This never gets old, and the greatest joy in ministry is to see spiritual sons and daughters birthed into the kingdom. I also enjoy traveling, although I don't do it as much as I used to. It's great to visit different towns and cities and see the beauty of America, and to visit different churches and meet new people, some of whom become good friends.

I am thankful for the wonderful friends we have made through the ministry, especially among pastors and the people who are ministry partners. Our closest friends are those we have met through the ministry.

It can be a challenge to be widely-recognized, so it is good to have close friends who are true friends and not just people who want to be around you because of television. A minister and his family often live in a glass house, meaning that their actions and words are observed and judged by others. This is especially true with someone who is known nationally or globally. For example, on the plane during one of Perry's Holy Land tours, a movie came on the screen that had offensive language. Perry took off his head set and didn't watch it. Later a woman in the back said, "I was watching him to see if he was going to watch that movie. If he had, I would have lost confidence in his ministry."

In a restaurant, people watch how the minister treats the servers, even looking to see what kind of tip he leaves. We have been eating out, when an unknown person near us would pull out a phone and begin taping us as we ate and talked to one another.

There is good with the bad, though. We have been traveling and had strangers come up to us and tell Perry how much they enjoy the Manna-fest program. With the complaints most well-known ministers must deal with, it is a pleasant surprise to have strangers give you a compliment.

We lose our privacy, but it's something we have to deal with because it comes with the territory. We live in public as we do in private, so there is nothing for us to hide. What you see is what you get.

Another thing I enjoy is being able to try foods and restaurants from different parts of the country. I like to cook, so I enjoy sampling local cuisines and knowing how different foods are prepared. Our whole family enjoys seafood, especially anything prepared with a Cajun touch. Food can be a temptation—especially chocolate. Yes, we can be tempted with food. Remember that Eve was temped with fruit from a tree, and Jesus was tempted with turning the stones into bread after He had been on a long fast. People don't always eat for nourishment alone, especially when there is food in abundance. Sometimes they eat out of stress or habit. For people who enjoy good food, it can be a challenge to discipline ourselves in that area.

One thing I do not enjoy that Perry and both our children eat is sushi. But I do enjoy oriental food, so while he and the kids dig into their rolls of fish and seaweed, I stick with stir-fry. I prefer food that doesn't look or taste like it walked straight out of the ocean and onto your plate.

Question: Do you think it is wrong to use birth control pills? Being from a Catholic background, I was taught that this form of birth control is wrong.

Answer: This is a sensitive subject for many people. Some believe that any type of birth control is wrong because it interferes with the natural plan of God for the family. Perry's dad had twelve brothers and sisters, ten of whom survived to adulthood. Years ago, families were large, and this was almost a necessity when people lived on farms. When people moved away from rural areas and had no family close by, when the cost of living increased, and when both couples started working, people began to limit the number of children they had.

I personally think that taking birth control pills is one of those areas where a woman must do as Philippians 2:12 says, and work out your own salvation with fear and trembling. If you have questions about this, study all you can about birth control and pray about it. If your conscience tells you not to use birth control, then don't. I have known people who had many children—one a year, it seemed—and were able to support and even homeschool all of them. Large families tend to be very close to each other, and the children mature faster. Older children will help care for younger children, and all are taught to pitch in and assist with chores. God will give people the grace and ability to handle large families, even though most tend to think they could never do it.

For any woman who stays on birth control pills long term, and especially if you are taking them after age forty, be sure you have yearly checkups. Doctors suggest that being on birth control pills after age forty could trigger cancer.

So the bottom line is, for any woman who is uncertain about this issue of birth control, you should discuss it with your husband, pray about it, and be in agreement.

Question: What is the most difficult situation you have gone through personally that is not ministry-related?

Answer: There were several difficult seasons in my life. They include struggles that one of our children has gone through, which is a weight for any parent. We always want the best for our children. Watching my mother age and experience physical difficulty has been hard. We saw Perry's dad pass away, unable to eat or drink anything for a few days before he died, as his organs were shutting down. It is emotionally difficult to see those you love suffer, especially when you know they are nearing the end of their life.

One of the saddest times for me over the years was when my best friend from Alabama, Tracy Davis, was killed in a car accident in January of 1990. An 18-wheeler pulled into her lane and her car ended up under the truck. An eye witnesses told the paramedics that there were two people in the front seat—one driving and one in the passenger's seat. Yet Tracy was alone in the car. We believe the second person was an angel of the Lord coming for her.

Recently we were going through some old letters and I found the last card she sent me. It was hard to lose a friend in such a horrible manner, and at such a young age. But we know she is with the Lord and that is always a comfort. The death of a close friend or family member is a difficult experience for anyone. We eventually expect our aging parents to pass away, but not a child or someone in the early stages of life's journey.

Question: Do you and your husband ever fuss and fight? People have a perception that ministers and their wives are perfect and seldom have disagreements, or that they walk in Divine and perfect love that prevents them from having arguments.

Answer: I'm sure there are a few people who assume that we never disagree or fuss. We have married friends who say, "My husband and I never have disagreements or arguments." I wonder if they ever talk to each other because, if you speak, at some point you will disagree and fuss about it.

Jesus was love and perfection, but He rebuked the Pharisees and overthrew the tables of the money changers. Paul and Barnabas were companions in ministry who had such a disagreement that they went their separate ways. They were not husband and wife, of course, but this reveals that anger or disagreement can happen, even among ministers and righteous people.

Perry and I have disagreements from time to time, as all married couples do. The argument is often over someone else we are dealing with rather than us personally, and we argue because we have a difference of opinion about the way something should be handled. We have never fought in the sense of physically fighting. Perry is quick to speak and he thinks out loud, which means he might say something and have to come back later and apologize for his words, his temper, or his tone of voice.

Before we were married, we made an agreement that we would not go to bed angry with each other. We would make things right before we went to bed, so that if one of us passed away in the night, our last memory would not be of anger or disagreement. It is better to have a last memory of saying or hearing, "I love you."

On one occasion we had an argument before church. While the pastor was praying, Perry came off the platform and said, "I'm not preaching until you forgive me." I said, "You silly goose, I forgive you. Go preach."

Most of our disagreements last only a short time. We resolve them and move forward. As a believer, the Bible tells us, "Be angry and do not sin, and do not let the sun go down on your wrath" (Eph. 4:26). We should do our best to resolve disagreements immediately instead of letting things simmer and turn into anger and forgiveness.

Question: It is evident from Internet blogs and other sources that some people don't like your husband's ministry. One preacher who has a radio and television program will call his name and says he is a heretic. Another man who claims he is an online pastor is even worse. How do you handle the criticism?

Answer: It's been said that if you are criticized by someone, or if they personally attack you, don't waste time defending yourself because your friends don't need it and your enemies won't receive it. Personal opinions are like noses—everybody has one.

Most critics do not personally know Perry and have never sat under his ministry. They form opinions based on rumors, and then they state their opinion as fact. People criticize something he teaches without ever listening to the entire teaching in context. Other people criticize because they do not believe something he teaches. For example, he is often criticized by those who do not believe in the baptism of the Holy Spirit or the gifts of the Spirit, so anybody who teaches those things becomes a false teacher or a heretic in their eyes. Others think the Old Testament should not be taught today, unless it is a story they selectively choose to preach.

We have heard some ridiculous rumors about Perry. One minister who calls Perry a heretic also calls almost everybody else on television a heretic. He believes he is the only person preaching truth.

It is nearly impossible to defend oneself from bitter, jealous, angry, critical, or unbelieving people and preachers. When you try to do so, you learn that it is a waste of time.

It still frustrates me, though, when people who do not even know us spread lies and rumors, or criticize a teaching just because they don't believe the whole Bible. But eventually the truth will emerge. The Lord will confirm Perry's teachings through results at the altars and fruit of the ministry.

In this season, when there is a clash between two kingdoms, you cannot believe everything you hear from people on the Internet, or even from ministers who claim to be the sole source of biblical truth. Don't get your information from the pit bulls of Christianity. Some people think they are called to be watchdogs, but in reality they are biting and spreading spiritual rabies within the body of Christ.

Question: Divorce is just as high among Christians as among unbelievers. Even ministers experience divorce. What are the keys to maintaining a strong marriage?

Answer: I am thankful that it has not been a struggle for Perry and me to maintain a strong marriage. First, God put us together, meaning that we married the person God chose for us, rather than choosing the person we wanted and expecting God to bless our choice. Perry and I are best friends, in addition to being husband and wife. If people allow God to choose their spouse, and if they keep God first, they will have a strong marriage.

One key is to never lose that "first love" feeling. Remember what you loved about each other in the beginning. Don't let the flame of love die. The ease with which people can get a divorce causes them to give up on their marriage too quickly.

This took years of discipline, but Perry had to learn to separate ministry work from home and relaxation. I try to make sure he does not bring the ministry cares into the house after work. It is important that people—and this can be especially difficult for men—to separate work from home.

Make time for each other. Forget the cares of life for a while and do something to relax with your spouse and family. We take more mini-vacations than we used to. So take a day here and there, and just go for a drive in the mountains, have a picnic, or visit a town or city that you've wanted to experience.

Most marriages have problems because there is a communication breakdown. A man can hear the words his wife is speaking, but not hear what she is really saying. I call it hearing but not listening. Hearing captures words, but listening causes you to respond to those words. Sometimes you can't hear each other for talking over each other, and you are preparing your next statement instead of listening to what your spouse is trying to say. Learn to skillfully communicate.

A marriage is like a nice car; it needs to be serviced occasionally to keep it in tip-top shape. Oil needs to be changed, tires need to be rotated, and the car needs regular maintenance. If you avoid taking care of maintenance, eventually there will be damage to the vehicle. Lack of maintenance can even lead to wrecks. Likewise, if you don't give special attention to your marriage and practice occasional maintenance, you will find yourself in a storm that could lead to a head-on collision with your companion.

Pay attention to the little things that matter to you both. Don't be selfish; marriage is not all about you and your needs. Don't have two heads and no heart—meaning that everything is rational, but there is no love or affection. And don't have two hearts and no head, meaning that marriage is all about affection with no common sense. Marriage takes two heads and two hearts united as one.

If you sense that your marriage is about to have a flat tire, then stop what you are doing and spend some quality time with your companion, away from the clamor and the hustle and bustle of life, so you can get things straightened out.

Finally, we know of some minister friends who came under an attack of the enemy that effected their marriage and family. In many instances, the root of the problem was physical and spiritual burn-out. They became too busy to pray, fast, and spend time in the quiet place before the Lord. When business becomes busy-ness, then ministry is no longer a joy. Sometimes you need to take time away from the busyness and renew your mind and marriage.

As a couple ages, maturity causes them to love one another in a different way. In the beginning was an attraction that pulled you together like a magnet. Later, you focus on the qualities of the person. But age brings a depth of maturity and an abiding love that is as firm as a mountain of rock. This love grows from the feeling of cherishing and admiring one another. The longer you are married, the more you will develop this kind of love for each other.

Question: From your travels and life experiences, what are some things you would tell a young women who is about to be married?

Answer: The first thing I would say is to be realistic about marriage and life. Cinderella is a wonderful fairy tale, but life and marriage are not a fantasy; they are reality. While dating, you are on your best behavior. You always look your best, smile, laugh, and put on a happy face. Then after your dream wedding, you will wake up the next morning and look a whole lot different. You will look this way each morning for years to come. Then once your husband has caught you, he knows he can relax and not do all those things he did to catch you. That is the reality.

Build your hopes on reality and not on fantasy or romance novel expectations. Traditional wedding vows say, for better or for worse, for rich or for poor, in sickness and in health, until we are parted by death. We enjoy the season when things are better, rich, and healthy. But it's the worse, poor, and sick that tempts a person to run away from his or her vows.

Always remember that marriage should be a life-long commitment. Never enter into marriage with the attitude that, if things don't work out as planned, you will divorce the person and then move on to the next assignment. Divorce and remarriage is common today and is accepted in our culture as a way to escape conflict with your spouse. But marriage is a covenant, and it should never be entered into with the divorce option on the table. There will be challenges, disagreements, and frustrations. But all of that can be worked through to bring resolution to each problem and situation.

Your marriage must be built upon love and not just emotion. When teenagers "fall in love," they might be experiencing lust and not love. At such a young age, they are unable to discern between the rush of chemicals in their brain that make them feel good, versus the true love that desires to build a life together. When a young girl says, "I saw him and it was love at first sight," it is really attraction at first sight. Love is not just a feeling in the flesh. It is a desire to honor and serve another, while sacrificing your own desires. It is 1 Corinthians 13 in action.

When you look at the one you want to marry, ask yourself if you will still love him when he no longer has that handsome face. Will you remain faithful to him in good and bad times? Will he remain faithful to you? Marriage is a wonderful blessing when you wait to marry the mate God chose for you. There is nothing like the joy of becoming one, having children, maturing, and building a life together. If you can do this, you will always have the spark of attraction and affection for each other that you had in the very beginning.

Question: What are your plans for ministry in the future? When do you plan on retiring? If something happens to Perry, who will take over the ministry and will it continue to operate as it does now?

Answer: The long term plans for Perry are to finish the study Bible, build a youth camp facility, and start a Leadership Training Center for youth. Both of us believe that we should occupy until the Lord comes, work as though Christ could return today, but plan as though He may not return in our lifetime.

As far as retiring, that is not in the picture and we have not discussed a particular time that we want to retire. We are going to work until the return of the Lord or until we are physically unable to continue, whichever comes first. Hopefully, we will both live long enough to see the return of Christ.

We have both invested our lives into the VOE and OCI ministries and we are aware that they must continue in the event that the Lord calls Perry home. Without a plan in advance, these ministries could be left in disarray. Our Board of Directors has discussed possible plans with us, because it is important to have those plans in place.

As far as who will step in our shoes, we believe that when the time comes, the Lord will already have that arranged and everything in place. We would love to see both of our children connected to the ministry and working for the Lord; but even if that does not happen, spiritual sons and daughters are coming along behind Perry who will fulfill God's future purposes, including the advancement of the Kingdom of God through the VOE and OCI ministries.

So at this point we plan to be here, together, to fulfill God's will for these ministries. When the time comes for a transition, then the Lord will have in place all those whom He desires to take the ministry forward.

From a personal standpoint, we have an irrevocable trust that will distribute personal assets to the children and to the people who will be responsible for caring for the children if they are unmarried at the time of our deaths. It is important for everybody to have an updated will or a trust. If you do not, the state will determine who receives your assets when you die. When Bea Ogle worked in a bank, she saw relatives come into the bank after a parent's death and demand access to accounts and safe deposit boxes. Sometimes a fight would break out as each one claimed to be the heir.

Perry and I both have God-given assignments to finish, and we trust God that He will allow us to fulfill them. Our future is in God's hands, so beyond the wisdom of preparation, we do not worry about it. When that time comes, people will be in place to carry on the ministry.

Question: How have you been able to build buildings, pay airtime for the Manna-fest program, and meet all the obligations of the ministry without sending out letters and continually asking for donations?

Answer: The primary reason we do not sent out letters asking for ministry offerings is because of a word Perry received when he was eighteen. The Holy Spirit instructed him not to send out letters asking for offerings, as the Lord would help him pay for whatever He directed him to do. We do not think badly about any ministry that does send letters regularly asking for support. But for us, we have a specific word that we are not to do this. Perry has followed this since 1977.

The way Perry stays in touch with people about our projects is through the Voice of Evangelism magazine, and by giving an update each month on CD through the message of the month. Both methods simply inform friends and partners of the most recent word of the Lord and the ministry related projects they can support. There are partners who support us regularly, and they are a tremendous blessing to help us continue with the ministries.

It has been a blessing and a miracle to watch the Lord provide much-needed finances to purchase property and construct three ministry facilities, staff the ministries, and provide for television air time. We believe that the secret to God's blessings is obedience. We do what He instructs us to do, and Perry preaches the messages that God instructs him to preach.

During a controversial television series, many people said he was legalistic for his stand on an issue and they complained about the messages. He told the staff, "We might as well prepare for the ministry to take a financial hit, because this message is not popular and it will turn a lot of people off." But during that series, the ministry received the largest donation in its history.

God is faithful to His Word. And God expects us to be obedient to Him instead of to man. God blesses obedience; it is the spiritual weapon that Satan fears the most.

Question: What is your greatest fear, either about life or ministry? Have there been circumstances that caused you to have fear?

Answer: I cannot think of an area, either in my life or the ministry, in which I battle fear. There might occasionally be a circumstance that arises and fear will attempt to enter (such as when Jonathan was not in the hotel room and when I was told I had cancer). In life, something such as an accident or a negative health report can cause fear to try to take hold in your mind.

There were a few times when a circumstance caused me to think the worst. One incident happened years ago after Jonathan was born. Perry and Charlie traveled in our van from Cleveland to Chattanooga (which is about thirty miles) to minister at the Bible Teaching Center. They left the house about five o'clock p.m. and the service began at seven o'clock. At seven o'clock I received a call from Rick Towe, the administrator of the church, asking if Perry remembered he was preaching that night. I told Rick that he left two hours ago.

Fear suddenly gripped me, as I began to imagine that Perry and Charlie must have been in an accident on the interstate. This was before the days of cell phones, so there was no way of knowing. Rick called back half an hour later and asked if I had heard from anyone. I had not. He said, "Someone who got here late said there was a wreck on the interstate with a white van, but they didn't know who was in the vehicle." My heart sank and even greater fear swept over me, since they were driving a white van!

At that moment, this thought came to me: "You have been given a son because God knew your husband would be killed." This thought created a surge of fear and I started crying. I began to pray that, whatever had happened, God would help Perry and Charlie. If they had been involved in an accident, I asked that the Lord not allow either of them to be physically harmed. I prayed intently as this spirit of fear swept over me, leaving me numb and filled with anxiety. All circumstances seemed to point to an accident—at least in my mind.

Eight o'clock arrived and they still were not at the church. More time passed with no word from anyone. With each minute, I began to think about what I would do without Perry, and how that, if he had been involved in a tragic accident, he would never see his son grow up.

I also knew that I had to take control of these thoughts because there was no evidence anything had happened. Perhaps they were stuck in traffic as a result of the accident someone had in a similar white van.

It was nearly eight-thirty when the phone rang. My heart raced. It was Rick Towe saying they had made it safely and both were fine. A white van was involved in the accident, but it was not our van. However, they had been stuck in traffic for hours with no way to call anybody. The relief lifted the fear.

Simple things can bring fear. When we lived in our first home, located at the edge of a small forest of trees, I heard a loud banging noise coming from the front porch. I thought somebody was trying to break in the door. I was alone at the time and had no way of physically defending myself. One reason I had that fear was because our home had been broken into one time while we were out of town, so naturally that was in the back of my mind. But the fear went away once

I realized the screen door had not closed and the wind was blowing against it, causing the door to bang against the doorframe. The enemy is the master of illusion, and he can create circumstances that appear to be real in your mind. While there are times when something is happening that justifiably creates an adrenaline surge of fear, there are more times when these fears are unfounded and they create unwanted stress.

Not all fear is bad, of course. Fear of being burned keeps us from sticking our hand into a flame, and fear of being hit by a car keeps children from running into the road. However, there is a spirit of fear that attempts to control our thoughts, causing us to live with worry and anxiety of what *could* happen. God has not given us a spirit of fear but of power, love, and a sound mind (2 Tim. 1:7). We give place to fear when we worry in advance about things because the circumstances are not as we perceive them to be.

I believe that the Lord is in charge of everything and our footsteps are ordered by Him. If you are in covenant with God and you persistently battle fear, you can be assured that it is not from God. Fear can open the door to attacks of the enemy, because as you walk in fear and begin to confess your fears, the enemy knows the areas in which you can be attacked. Fear is a weapon of the enemy that produces tormenting thoughts (1 John 4:18). Perfect love removes fear. Perfect love comes from understanding Christ's love for us and His willingness to protect, defend, and watch over us. He will shield us so that no weapon formed against us will prosper (Isa 54:17).

One of the greatest fears people have is the fear of dying and death. Perry and I have both asked each other what we would do if one of us passed away and the other was still here. We both know that, when it is time for us to depart, nothing can hold us here. Once a believer has gained confidence in Christ and freedom from the fear of death, no other fear can hold them captive.

Question: As a partner of the ministry, I heard Brother Perry explain to us the details of the future vision. What is *your* future vision, not only for your personal life, but also in the ministry? Do you have your own goals that you don't share with people?

Answer: My vision is completely connected to the vision of VOE and OCI. My ministry is to minister to my husband and family and to serve in whatever capacity I am needed in the ministry. I do not have my own vision, dream or agenda. I simply go with the flow. If Perry and I have conflicting visions, this is division; and where there is division, there is confusion. We have seen married couples in ministry who both have their own ministries, and some have gone their separate ways to minister according to their own itineraries and speaking engagements. Years later they found themselves separated or divorced.

I am not a minister or a speaker; I am a helper. My ministry is to encourage others and to live an example before them that they can follow. If the pre-teen and early teen girls are influenced by my life's examples, and they grow up desiring to follow Christ because of my spiritual influence, then I have fulfilled my ministry.

Any woman who is married to a man who is involved in the fivefold ministry (Eph. 4:11) must serve as a helper to her companion. A wife can make or break her husband's ministry. Her motive for marriage must be love for the man above love for the ministry. A woman cannot be enamored with the ministry and marry someone just because she wants to be part of that ministry. If she does that, she will end up disappointed or disillusioned, which will cause stress, strife, and division in the home. If you marry the man, your heart must be with him wherever he goes.

Question: I read your husband's book, *Dealing with Hindering Spirits,* about the attack with demonic spirits that he experienced as a teenager. Occasionally I have met others who had a similar experience. Have you ever encountered any type of visible demonic activity?

Answer: Most people who are actively doing something for the Lord know that the adversary is keenly aware of those who are pulling people from the pit of destruction and seeing them converted to the Lord. These people, who also spend much time in prayer and fasting, can tap into the unseen spirit realm and see both angelic and demonic beings. Fred Stone was sensitive to the spirit realm, and fasting and prayer sharpened his discernment. This is why all the gifts of the Spirit operated in his life.

The enemy perceives these kinds of people as a threat to the kingdom of darkness. With Perry, he would pray, fast, and engage in Bible study for hours every day, and he would sometimes experience these demonic attacks right before a major breakthrough in the ministry.

I confess that I'm glad I have never experienced some of the visible (and audible) supernatural manifestations that Perry has experienced over the years. At times he would say to me with frustration, "A demonic power was in the room last night, and I rebuked it. Did you sense anything?" I would simply say, "No, not a thing." At times he wondered why he could sense it and I didn't.

But there would really be no purpose for both of us to see something that he is already seeing and hearing. I would compare it to Elisha, who saw the horses and chariots of fire on the mountain, but his servant saw nothing. Only after Elisha prayed for the eyes of his servant to be opened did the servant see the supernatural heavenly protection that surrounded them (2 Kings 6:15-17). Many times the eyes and ears of a person are open in the natural but closed to the invisible realm. Perry's spirit is just more sensitive to these things than mine, and I am thankful for that. I have no desire to see a demonic manifestation or hear a voice in the night.

When you hear Perry describe what he has seen in the spirit realm, you realize what the Apostle Paul meant when he said that we are not in a battle with flesh and blood, but with principalities and powers of darkness (Eph. 6:12). The spiritual battles that Perry has encountered over the years are not necessarily your average encounter, but they are above the level of common testing (1 Cor. 10:13). However, the Holy Spirit will always help us overcome all obstacles that the adversary attempts to bring our way, and give us a path of escape and a road to victory.

Question: If Christ tarries and you should go to be with the Lord before His return, what would you like people to remember about you?

Answer: Perry often talks about leaving a legacy, or something in ministry that carries on long after a person has departed. I believe the vision for OCI and all projects connected to that dream are part of the ministry legacy that is being left for the next generation. As for me personally, I want to be remembered as a good wife and mother, and a person who cared about people. Most importantly, I want many lives to be touched and changed because I lived on this planet. Just as Perry, I desire to have an eternal reward that will never fade away.

CONCLUSION

Each year, visitors from various states walk through 70,000-square-feet of VOE office and studio space, and the 72,000 square foot OCI facility marveling at God's goodness. Many are new partners who have connected with the ministry after watching the Manna-fest telecast. Many are unaware of the early sacrifices and steps that were required to demonstrate our faithfulness to God and our determination to fulfill His will. It is that faithfulness and obedience that has brought us to the level of ministry we are now experiencing. We could not accomplish the things we do if it were not for the grace and blessings of God, and the people who support the ministry.

This book has highlighted my journey thus far. When you link with us as partners of the ministry, we have a book called, *We Are Not Finished Yet,* that we send you as a gift for your partnership. We thank God for our partners and friends. We don't see all of the future, and we don't know everything that is in store for us, for America, or for the world. No doubt there will be more bumps along the way, more trials of our faith, and more tests and victories to write about one day. We are still fighting the good fight of faith, still planting the seed for a spiritual harvest, and still running this race. We are not finished yet!